THE PRISCILLA REVELATION

and

THE DISCOVERY OF THE APPLE CONSTELLATION

THE PRISCILLA REVELATION

and

THE DISCOVERY OF THE APPLE CONSTELLATION

CAROLYN M. BEEHLER

EDITED BY DANA BEEHLER GOWARD

CONTENTS

Foreword..ix

Acknowledgments xi

Prologue..xiii

Chapter 1: Henri...1

Chapter 2: The Revelation! 7

Chapter 3: The Research Begins, and the Revelation Continues....13

Chapter 4: A Needed Break . . . Then More Discoveries................27

Chapter 5: My Diary in Rome, 1978.......................................35

Chapter 6: Home—Just the Beginning 59

Chapter 7: A Discovery 64

Chapter 8: Equal Rites for Women..70

Chapter 9: Continued Discovery 76

Chapter 10: Discovering More History 85

Chapter 11: God Doesn't Call the Qualified;
            He Qualifies the Called 91

Chapter 12: Back to Rome 95

Epilogue... 103

Letter from Henri...106

Notes 111

DISCOVERY

If we have seen what we were meant to see
guide our vision; grant that it may rise
in other times and places known to Thee
to dawn like light of day on other eyes.

If we have glimpsed a world that is to be
and then we die and we can do no more
defend the dream we dream because of Thee
and bring it safe to shore.

—Ruth Hoppin

FOREWORD

Carolyn was our mother. And it is hard for children to fully appreciate their parents being anything other than just being their parents. We three daughters—Bonnie, Amy, and me (Dana)—had the greatest love and affection for her. Yet during her lifetime, we never truly appreciated Mom's phenomenal spiritual encounter or her incredible accomplishment. She was just our mom.

But Carolyn was also an artist, with an artist's temperament and eye that saw life with a perspective different than most. My sisters and I had long experience with, and fondness for, Mom's eccentricities. We would often listen to her thoughts with bemused skepticism. Her story of Priscilla, an ancient biblical woman who called to her across time about authoring a book of the Bible, was a bit more involved than most. Still, we only half-listened. We were pleased that she had a project that seemed to keep her busy and in high spirits.

It wasn't until June 1980, when *Smithsonian* magazine published her discovery of an ancient sky chart in Priscilla's catacomb, that we finally began to sit up and take notice. Our artist mother, with her talent of seeing from different perspectives and her discerning eye, saw what, for almost two thousand years, others had missed. We were amazed that she, with only a high school education, had achieved so much. In Mom's quest to prove that a woman, Priscilla, had written a part of the New Testament, and with the help of Henri Nouwen, the famous theologian, she went to Rome to seek the answers. During her research there, she discovered a sky chart hidden in a fresco in a catacomb that pinpointed the date when the Christmas star appeared.

Mom tried many times to put her experiences into writing. There were numerous starts and stops, and she left many drafts behind when she passed away. She had high hopes, while she lived, that one of her daughters would take on the task and help tell her story. Yet the pressures of our own families and lives prevented us from making the attempt until years after her passing. Even then, Mom's drafts, notes, books, correspondence, and other references passed like a hot potato between the three sisters for several years. The job and privilege to take up the mantle finally settled with me, Dana, the middle daughter. This is our mom's true story. It is an account of her spiritual revelation, journey with Priscilla, and eventual discovery of the hidden sky chart showing the date of Christ's birth.

ACKNOWLEDGMENTS

We wish to thank these people who helped to make the discoveries in this book possible.

Mrs. Steven Berry (Carol); Dr. C. Arthur Bradley; Dean Charles "Kelly" H. Clark; Sr. Elizabeth Carroll; Mr. Roland Clement; Rabbi Arthur Chiel; Dr. Dorothy Durand; Pres. Francis de Salle Haffernen; Dir. Sophie Consagra; Sr. Joan Doing; Sr. Edward (SIDIC); Rev. Umberto Fasola; Sr. Maria Francesca; Rev. Donald Frazier; Rev. Elizabeth Frazier; Dr. Elisabeth Schüssler Fionenza; Prof. Margherita Guarducci; Dr. Dorrit Hoffleit; Rev. John Irvine; Susan Jaskot; Dr. Martha Leonard; Sr. Catherine Lafferty; Mrs. Reg. Marini (Gladys); Sr. Jane MacDermott; Mrs. Clinton MacMullen (Bea); Rev. Martin McCarthy, SJ; Prof. Alice Mulhern; Rev. Henri Nouwen; Mrs. Allen Neff (Edith); Sr. Charles Marie Parsons; Rt. Rev. Morgan Porteus; the Pizzuto Family; Dr. S. Dill Ripley; Rev. Daniel Sanders; Sr. Juanita Sacri; Dr. Harry R. Smythe; Dr. Joseph H. Taylor; Dr. Edward Thompson; Prof. Albert Vanhoye; Mr. John Wiley Jr.; Sister Wanda; Dean Colin Williams; Rev. Hans Wijngaard; Rev. William Woodhams; Photographer Bini; my patient husband, Daniel; and to our children, Bonnie, Dana, and Amy; and to the spirit of all who encouraged me.

PROLOGUE

God reveals himself not to the person who is self-sufficient
or self-righteous, but to the one whose mind is open, whose
will is receptive, and whose soul is humble.

—Unknown

East Lawn Cemetery had just turned off their sprinkler system after
watering the grass in preparation for the following day's funeral. The
grass was still wet and slippery as the funeral director and my daughters
supported me on my unsteady feet to view the soon-to-be grave site of
my husband, Daniel.

Dan had taken care of me night and day for the last four months
during a long, chronic illness. During those months, my muscles had
atrophied. But now it was not me but *he* who was gone. A classic
example of the exhausted caretaker succumbing to the arduous task of
caring too much. As I examined the grave site, I became overly curious
and stepped away from everyone to look closer. I quickly turned, and to
my surprise, I fell down onto the exact spot where Dan was to be buried!

"How's the view from down there, Mom?" asked one of my girls.
Humor can come at odd moments, a defense mechanism during tragedy.

Although pain shot through my foot, I shouted back "It's great!"
and silently said to Dan, "Look, hon, I got here before you, and I'm
okay." But I wasn't.

I arrived at the hospital emergency room a bit muddied up.
Surprisingly, one of the doctors on duty was a rheumatologist who
became more concerned about my chronic weakened condition than

my torn tendon. I felt life was truly unfair because after suffering for months and tiring my husband to his death with my care, it was only then the doctors finally diagnosed me with an autoimmune disease called polyarteritis nodosa. This inflammatory disease had allowed only a small amount of blood and oxygen to reach my muscles, and they were beginning to fail. There was a strong indication that if I had not gotten the medical attention at that time, I wouldn't have lasted for much longer. It was fortunate, or perhaps foreordained, that I fell in the cemetery and finally got the care I needed.

During the following weeks of recovery, I had ample time to mourn my husband and contemplate my own future. Foremost in my mind, though, was the past, thinking of all the wonderful opportunities I had experienced in my life. Out of all those blessings, there was one set of memories that stood out from all the rest, a period of several years that had changed my life forever.

I had been an artist, art instructor, wife, and mother. While I had extensive training as an artist, my academic education had ended after high school. And when it came to religion and spirituality, I was only an occasional holiday Christian. Yet I had one sudden and surprising religious experience that was life altering. It had taken me to people, places, and discoveries I never would have dreamed possible. My story is a strange one, yet I feel compelled to tell it. A revelation carried me on a spiritual journey of discovery that took me into the depths of the earth, up into the heavens, and to another dimension of living. It led me to hidden ancient treasures in art, science, history, and religion! With the help of some present-day earthly angels and the spiritual guidance of an ancient biblical woman, I was led in directions and connected to people who would help me on my way.

Incredible as it may seem, the sequence of events that dominated my life for those years was set in motion by a voice calling to me across the span of almost two thousand years. I had never studied parapsychology, nor was I a scholar or historian. Yet for some strange reason, a message from an ancient woman came to me clearly, with an urgency that stirred me deeply. I knew little about her life and the society in which she lived. I could place her vaguely as a figure known to some of the disciples in the New Testament. But at the time of my revelation, I could not discern any more than that. For some reason, I had been chosen to speak for this woman, and the more I resisted, the more firmly I was led into an unknown and thoroughly intriguing history and discoveries. How much of what occurred was coincidental? It is hard for me to believe that any of it was.

I have asked myself where this revelation or compulsion came from, and depending on my mood, one of two quotations came to mind. Either one could apply: "God moves in mysterious ways. His wonders to perform" or "Fools rush in where angels fear to tread." My own adventures were important only as they served to document a biblical woman's message, yet they had lifted my own life out of its normal pattern and into another dimension.

CHAPTER ONE

Henri

It was 1978 and I had been teaching art classes, mostly in watercolors, from my studio in New Haven, Connecticut, for several years. Teaching art had always been a pleasure for me. I found a very real satisfaction in helping my students, who came from a wide variety of backgrounds. Of late, exhibition of my own work had become less exciting than the challenge of helping others to develop their own artistic talents. In my classes, students and friends would make suggestions as to subjects they wished to study. One day I found myself being directed toward the study of religion in art.

It all began with a call from Reverend C. A. Bradley, the minister of the Church of the Redeemer in New Haven. He asked if I would be willing to teach a short art course in conjunction with a Bible course he was teaching.

The title of the course he wanted me to teach was the Spirituality of Religion in Art. This was inspired by a previous set of classes taught by Rev. Donald Frazier, an interim minister that had been serving during Rev. Bradley's sabbatical year. I had attended the previous course and assisted with some painting lessons.

Though I knew little about the Bible, I replied to Reverend Bradley's request in the affirmative. Already I was thinking how easy this would be. I would just have the class paint a simple biblical landscape. He then said that the related parallel Bible study course was The Letter to the Hebrews.

"No problem," said I. "Now isn't that in the Old Testament, right?"

After a long silence, and a clearing of his throat, he said, "No, Carolyn, it is not in there. It is in the New Testament. Do you think you can teach something like this, something that you are not familiar with?"

Our conversation was humorous, as well as a little embarrassing for me. I assured him that I would find it, read it, and would have no problem teaching it in parallel with his Bible study course. Everyone would go home with a lovely landscape painting. Enthusiastic about having a new subject to teach, I settled down to read The Letter to the Hebrews.

Moments later as I was flipping pages in the Bible, I found The Letter to the Hebrews in the New Testament, just where Reverend Bradley said it would be. When I searched in its text for something that could be used as a landscape for our Bible painting class, I found, to my surprise, there was none! There wasn't one reference to any kind of a landscape in the text. I sat there dumbfounded and discouraged. Who did I think I was, trying to conduct a biblical painting class?

I didn't know very much at all about this part of the Bible. What could I do? I would just have to go with what I did know, and that was colors. The only thing that came to my mind was to have my adult class paint a star with twelve points. The star points would each be a different color. The points would gradate through the color spectrum, starting at red, going clockwise, until ending at the twelfth color, red-purple. The star could represent the twelve tribes or the twelve apostles. Though this didn't really seem to have much to do with the content of The Letter to the Hebrews, at least it was a place to start. Finally, I thought, I could relax in my comfort zone, knowing how I would begin this religion in art class.

Classes started a few weeks later. The basics of color and watercolor techniques were the beginning lessons. Soon the lessons progressed to studying the text of The Letter to the Hebrews. Our discussions soon became more about theology than art.

One morning, a student of mine, Bea MacMullen, called to say she was going to hear Henri Nouwen, a Catholic priest, talk at the Mercy Center in Madison. She invited me to come along. I did not particularly care to hear a priest talk about sins or whatever they talked about. But my student insisted, saying Henri was as interested in art as I was, and his program was on the art of living. On the spur of the moment, I accepted her invitation.

We arrived at the gates to find the long twisted driveway lined with cars. When we arrived inside, there was another long line of people waiting to be seated. The din from the audience at the Mercy Center was electrified with anticipation to hear just this one man speak. I was impressed. I thought to myself, *All these people to hear one man speak? No choir, no organ music, just this man?*

My anticipation grew as a man stepped onto the stage. He wore glasses and a scratchy tweed jacket. Could this be our speaker, the priest? Father Henri Nouwen? He walked over to the lectern and did a most unusual thing. He lifted the lectern, turned, and carried it off stage! *He must be the custodian*, I thought, for he left a very empty stage, devoid of anything. But no, he returned and walked over to where the lectern had been and stood in its place! Not moving but staring out at all of us. Of course, we were all staring back at this lone figure. He stood there very tall and very still. He did not speak for many embarrassing moments until all sound ceased. We waited. The quiet seemed to bring him to life. He raised his head. His extralong fingers reached out in an imploring gesture. From the silence, a strange, heavily accented Dutch voice broke the silence.

"Now you will listen!" His first three words sounded to me like his own last name, Nouwen. "Did you do all that you planned to do today? Did you write your letters? Did you shop? Did you care for your home and others? Are you sure you did all that you should have done today? Did you leave time for God? No? Are you too busy being good?" He asked if we were filling out our lives with goodness by helping this one and that one, making every moment count. "Stop!" he shouted. "Empty yourself, for how can God enter if you have left no time or space for him? Let us take a few minutes of what is left of our day for God."

He looked at his watch and asked us to bow our heads. In less than a minute, he again looked at his watch and said, "Very well, let's try for half a minute. There, we have done it! Now let us get on to living in God's world and enjoying his gift of life that he gave you! Don't be so busy trying to do good works that you left no time to enjoy him. He loves you." He continued speaking about the interruptions in our lives and the challenges we face when we reach our goal in life. He said we would look back on our lives and find that it was the interruptions that were our life. I found his comments that day profound and very thought provoking.

Afterward, Bea, my student-friend, introduced me to Henri Nouwen. His presence was so powerful that I felt self-conscious and responded awkwardly to the introduction with some senseless comment, immediately regretting it. I went home thoroughly disappointed with myself. I had known other priests, so it was not his religious status that awed me. It was, rather, his charisma, which was so overpowering. Regretfully, I realized that our paths were not likely to ever cross again. Little did I know what destiny had planned.

The following morning I got a call from Rev. Donald Frazier, who was now at the Yale Divinity School, inviting me to visit him at his office. He had a gift for me in appreciation for a painting I had done for him. While in his office, we heard the insistent chiming of the divinity school's choral bells. It created a mood and inspired us to attend Mass. Though I lived close to Yale University, this was the first time I had been to the divinity school chapel. The atmosphere had a pleasant ecumenical feeling—a Congregational minister and I, an Episcopalian, attending a Roman Catholic Mass. The combination was beautiful.

There were banners hanging from this dignified structure, giving it a youthful and colorful twist. It was when my eyes turned away from the decorations that I noticed the priest, Henri Nouwen. After the Mass, Donald introduced me to Henri, but Henri gave no indication that he had just met me the previous night. I assumed he probably did not remember.

A few days later, I was invited to attend the ordination of a woman at the Choate school in Wallingford, Connecticut. This repeated involvement with persons of the cloth seemed sudden and bewildering, especially for me, since I did not consider myself as anything other than an occasional church-service attendee. But I accepted this invitation with curiosity.

It was a brisk, clear late autumn day when I slid into the end of a pew just in time to watch the procession and count the faces as they passed. Thirty-five ministers, priests, and rabbis marched by. There was Reverend Frazier, Reverend Dr. C. A. Bradley, who had invited me, and a few more familiar faces. And one that was becoming more familiar, Father Henri Nouwen! I thought to myself, *He sure gets around . . . or was it me?*

I was invited to attend the reception afterward. As I stepped into the old Victorian house, I was swept along in a crowd and stopped at the side of the Dutch priest who had entered my life for the third time that week. This time he recognized me, but the din of voices made our conversation difficult.

I was filled with questions and remember saying to him, "I have so much I want to say to you!"

He leaned his face into mine, almost nose to nose, invading my personal space, and said, "Yes? Well, come see me Monday morning after class at the Yale Divinity School." It was at that point I became aware that I knew very little about this man.

After attending one of my rare church-service visits on Sunday, I asked our minister if he knew of Henri Nouwen, because I had an appointment with him for the next day. Reverend Bradley assured me he did know of him and said, "Before you meet with him, I think you should read one of his books." In the church library, he found Henri Nouwen's *The Genesee Diary*, and I spent the rest of the day reading it.

The book told of his days and doubts in the Trappist monastery at Genesee, New York. It was a deeply moving and personal work. His writing revealed his vulnerability, which reached into my soul. In the middle of the book, he described a painting hanging on the monastery wall that he could not forget. The painting was an artist's interpretation of Henry Thoreau's philosophy:

> Why should we be in such haste to succeed and in such desperate enterprises? If a man does not keep pace with his companions, perhaps it is because he hears a different drummer. Let him step to the music which he hears, however measured or far away.

He also spoke about a book titled *Thomas Merton: A Different Drummer* by Robert J. Voigt.

I was taken aback, for I too liked Henry Thoreau's quote and had painted my interpretation of it four years before, in June of 1974—in the same year Henri had seen the monastery painting with the same theme.

Reading this made me realize there seemed to be a continued series of coincidences of the Spirit and timing between Henri and me. My painting had been leaning against my studio wall, unsold, for many years. I had enjoyed painting it and wondered why it did not appeal to any buyers. The painting was of a frog vigorously playing drums at his own pace, while several other frogs were trying to jump out of the painting to escape from the drumming. This frog was a different drummer. Frogs don't play drums, but this one didn't know that. Unbeknownst to me, I must have painted this for Henri before I knew he existed. I knew that this painting was meant for him. I packed it into the trunk of the car.

When I arrived to meet with Henri the next day, the rain was pouring down. It didn't seem to dampen our spirits, for we found ourselves having so much to say, stopping only long enough to exchange gifts. It was still raining when I pulled the painting from the car, but Henri did not seem to notice. Henri's response to my gift was welcoming, like a delighted child. It was more than I expected as he understood its double meaning and laughingly accepted it.

He sat on the hood of the car and expounded on the virtues of art in religion. He had my full attention except for the trouble of seeing through my wet eyeglasses and my awareness that my watercolor was in danger of being destroyed by the rain. He finally realized it too, took me back inside, and sat me down in his office. As we talked, he stacked copies of his books on a desk. Opening each book, he wrote a special message inside and generously loaded my arms with them. When we said good-bye, there were no assurances we would ever meet again. The events of my life had been ordered so strangely in the past week. I felt convinced that this man had been brought into my life for some purpose—a purpose not yet revealed.

CHAPTER TWO

The Revelation!

God is best known by revelation, not explanation.[1]

As the weeks passed, my art class and I continued to read and study The Letter to the Hebrews. Initially, I found the reading rather slow and dull. One day as I was alone and preparing for class, I found it difficult to concentrate, and my thoughts began to wander. I tried to focus on my lesson plan. As I attempted to concentrate, I became increasingly frustrated and confused. My mind suddenly felt an emptiness, a hollow feeling of *nothingness*. I felt completely empty. I asked myself, "Does one feel emptiness, or does the very feeling of emptiness mean that there is really something within me?"

I sensed that this empty feeling was important. I thought, *Something needs this space of nothing in order for it to expand. The empty space provides and allows room for the energy of something else to enter.* Henri's words, when I first met him, echoed in my head: "Empty yourself, for how can God enter if you have no time or space for him." I stopped and waited with a sense of timelessness. I did not know what to expect but was conscious that I needed to be open to whatever was to come. There was an air of anticipation. All at once, something filled me!

A whirlwind rush of energy came up from the pages I had been reading. It ran through me. It seemed to possess me. I felt I was imploding and exploding at the same time. Knowledge that went beyond experience became part of me. I felt an intellect and knew things I could not possibly know! It was a power or faculty of knowing without conscious reasoning. It started coming faster and faster.

I had never before experienced this kind of event, and I don't believe many other people have. It felt as though a rushing wave of knowledge far beyond my frame of reference came pouring into my mind so quickly that there was no time to question its source. How did one attempt to capture these new thoughts? I grabbed a pen and began to write it all down, thinking it would be gone before I could finish. But the flowing rush of knowledge did not go away. Instead, it was my own hand that could not keep up with the speed of it invading my mind and body.

Knowledge was coming faster than I was capable of writing. I didn't even try to number the pages. How could I have known that this revelation would take so many pieces of paper! The most exciting part of it for me was that the knowledge being revealed was about the history of Christianity, and it was in a language that I knew—art!

On a nearby table was a tape recorder with a Christmas tape from one of my daughters, but hastily I erased it. I started speaking into it as another way to capture this new knowledge. My hand was writing something different from what I was saying into the tape recorder. I was split in two. Information was spilling forth.

A torrent of new ideas continued to form even as I spoke. I ran upstairs to my art studio to revisit the color spectrum star I had created for my classes. I remembered that God often reaches us through the subject we know best. For me, it was color.

This revelation was saying, "Religion in art is a conception, a creation, a revelation, a reflection . . . a total experience in each lesson, a never-to-be-repeated moment . . . a fulfillment. Art is a religious experience at a particular moment in an artist's life as the thought is *conceived,* to the stroking of the paint, through *creation* of the picture, which *reveals* the soul of the artist, until its *reflection* on the viewer. All of life too is a conception, a creation, a revelation, and a reflection."

As I looked at the color spectrum star, a new meaning emerged from it. I now understood even more the interrelationship of colors and how they related to Christianity. Each color has its own properties, just as each of us is our own unique self. Yet part of each color is a reflection of the color next to it, just as we too, in part, reflect those around us. Orange is orange only because it is part yellow and part of its other neighbor, red. We are like the color orange, though we choose how light or dark a shade we become by the direction in which we live our lives. This principle of reflectivity also holds true for all the other colors, except for the three primary colors—blue, red, and yellow. These primary colors became, for me, the trinity of pure color.

I now saw this trinity of color living within us:

o   God, the Creator, the Synchronization, the Order, the Rhythm of the Universe, is the color *blue.*

o   The Son, the Mediator, the Teacher, the Humanitarian, is *red.*

o   The Holy Ghost, the Spirit, the Substance hoped for taking us beyond our capabilities, is the color *yellow.*

Mixing these three primary colors creates all twelve colors in our spectrum!

Twelve colors expand from the three, and twelve apostles sent as his messengers to spread the new covenant from the Trinity. I now understood with clarity the Lord sending the rainbow as a symbol of hope.

This twelve-pointed color spectrum star could also represent the new covenant as set forth in The Letter to the Hebrews. Twelve new

Color Spectrum Star

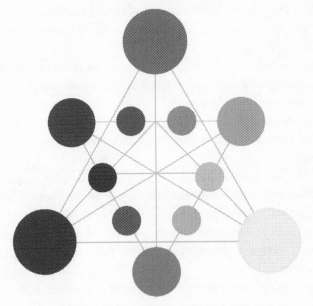

see back cover for color version

9

positive commandments to live by. Through the revelation, I had a new understanding. The colors in the star took on a whole new meaning and importance.

I turned again to reading The Letter to the Hebrews, feeling that if indeed God had revealed to me a way to view religion through art, he might also give me greater insight into this particular portion of the New Testament, written by some unidentified disciple almost two thousand years ago. Again, I had a feeling of anticipation that something was there, waiting for me to discover it. Where was God leading me? And why me?

As I read on, suddenly the overwhelming revelation became very clear to me. Something had been hidden for many centuries: a *woman* had written The Letter to the Hebrews! "Impossible," I told myself. Scholars would have discovered and documented this long ago if it were true. And yet? Again, that feeling of all-encompassing certainty took possession of me. A woman *did* write The Letter to the Hebrews. I shook with wonder. "My God, how can this be proved?" I prayed, "Show me the way to prove it to a doubting world and to a doubting me!"

Where does one start on such a monumental task? I had no training in historical research or any knowledge of the original language in which the New Testament was written. I was neither a Bible student nor a scholar in any sense. Had God planned to reveal the authorship of this particular letter at a point in time when the world could accept the writings of a woman without its content and credibility being jeopardized? When and how had I been prepared to receive this revelation? Or was it because I was just open and receptive enough at the right time in the right place? Since then, people have asked, "Why you?" and I have replied, "Yes, why me? If I were God, I wouldn't have chosen me. I should have been the last person in history to receive this assignment."

I questioned myself, reread the chapter, and thought maybe I was seeing femininity in it because of my own feminine perspective. Could a woman have written this part of the Bible? And why should I care? This insight was not something that I had wanted. Yet I could sense that a strong feminine spirit had sent this knowledge. Why had I been chosen to receive it?

To answer my questions, I thought about how, in the twentieth century, many women are free to speak out in the roles they choose.

This woman was saying to me, in her thoughts and spirit, "Now, my time has come." I knew the world was ready to accept that two thousand years ago a woman had the intellect and wisdom and was capable of communicating so fluently.

Continuing to read in my King James Bible, I searched for evidence of the female in the text and hints of her identity. The letter speaks in many feminine analogies, referring many times to women, children, and milk.

Here are some examples:[2]

- "And again, I will put my trust in Him. And again, *Behold I and the children which God hath given me*" (Heb. 2:13).
- "*Forasmuch then as the children are partakers of flesh and blood*, he also himself likewise took part of the same" (Heb. 2:14).
- "*For every one that useth milk is* unskillful in the word of righteousness: *for he is a babe*" (Heb. 5:13).
- "*Through faith also Sara herself received strength to conceive seed, and was delivered of a child when she was past age*, because she judged him faithful who had promised" (Heb. 11:11).
- "*Women receive their dead raised to life again:* and others were tortured, and not accepting deliverance; that they might obtain a better resurrection" (Heb. 11:35).

Was I going to be an instrument, destined to identify the unknown writer of Hebrews? Certainly, I did not share the same cultural limitations she had. Her message was very clear to me: "Unveil the mystery of the author of The Letter to the Hebrews, and let the world know that I wrote." But I came to realize The Letter to the Hebrews was one of the unsigned New Testament letters. I understood that no one was sure about its authorship. That fact took on a new significance.

Proving that a woman wrote The Letter to the Hebrews would be a daunting task. I had thought that two thousand years ago, women were not permitted to teach, nor were they allowed to write any kind of learned documents. The author of The Letter to the Hebrews prepared the text well to preserve her anonymity. This must have been necessary to ensure this precious doctrine would be accepted. Perhaps, if it had become known that it was written by a woman, it would not have survived as part of the Bible for two thousand years. At some point during the canon's many revisions and edits, it would have been rejected. Sadly, she could not sign her own work. Any great man of that time would have been proud to sign his name to this masterpiece. And yet she couldn't entirely mask her femininity and may not have wanted to. She left clues in the text, hoping someday to be recognized as the author of this doctrine—a doctrine for faithful Christian living.

CHAPTER THREE

The Research Begins, and the Revelation Continues

My attempt at "formal" research took me to the Yale Divinity School Library. I stared at the many volumes, and though I was highly motivated, I had no clear direction as how to start my search. I picked up *The Abingdon Bible Commentary*. As I settled down to read, an incredible quiet surrounded me, as if the entire world were shut out. Leafing through the commentary, I learned that there had always been controversy over the authorship of Hebrews,[3] and the issue was still unsettled. The author was still a mystery! This certainly left the door open for my nomination of a woman. But who?

Scholars had, in various writings, attributed it to Apollos, Barnabas, Clement, Silas, Philip, Priscilla and Aquila, Luke, and Paul. It was at one time called the Epistle of Paul to the Hebrews, but new Bible editions no longer used this title. In spite of the uncertainty, and a long list of possible candidates, for two thousand years the men who decided which books should be in the Bible had kept Paul's name as the author. Why? Even I, a laywoman, could see that Paul's style of writing was quite different from that of The Letter to the Hebrews. I grew angry at the male-dominated church culture that called for blind faith while at the same time minimizing the contributions of women. It was time for such false traditions to be challenged. Paul certainly would not have wanted credit for something he did not do. While crediting Paul had preserved the wisdom through the ages until now, it was time for the truth to be told. A woman had written The Letter to the Hebrews.

My inexperienced research continued to be driven by an encouraging spirit. I could not explain it except as a testament to a living spirit at work. I was driven to seek answers. As part of my journey, I sought more wisdom from great scholars in theology and history. Who did they think was the author?

Martin Luther (AD 1483–1546)was sure that it was Apollos, or a man of similar scriptural thought and background. He realized that in the absence of any definite evidence, this was simply a hypothesis.[4] When I examined Apollos as potential author and read of his self-assuredness, I thought him an unlikely choice. For one reason, The Letter to the Hebrews ends with an apology. Not a sign of someone filled with self-assurance.

Other great scholars who wrote on this subject included the following:

Tertullian (c.155/160–220), a Roman theologian, also believed that Barnabas wrote it. Tertullian believed in the sacrificial system. This undoubtedly made him favorably disposed toward Barnabas, who was a Levite and, therefore, practiced sacrifice. The sacrificial system was a way of dealing with guilt, mostly through burning animals on the altar. Tertullian also practiced Montanism, which taught that Christians should seek persecution and not run away from it.[5] Barnabas also believed that persecution was part of the Christian journey. If he had been the author of The Letter to the Hebrews, he would not have omitted his signature as a way of avoiding persecution.

Origen (c. 185–254) was an early Christian Alexandrian scholar and theologian. At one time, he thought Barnabas was the author. A woman as the author would probably have been inconceivable to Origen. Not only did he live in a traditional male-dominated culture, his attitude toward sex was such that he castrated himself as a matter of ritual purification. His final conclusion on the question of authorship was thus, "The ideas were Paul's but that The Letter was written by a disciple of Paul and then finally admitted only God could identify the inspired writer."[6]

St. Clement of Alexandria (c. 150–211/215) had referred to The Letter in his writing. He believed it was written by Paul and had been translated into Greek by Luke.[7]

Jerome (c. 347–419/420), an Illyrian priest, translator of the Bible to Latin,[8] and apologist, says about the writer to the Hebrews, "We must admit that the epistle written to the Hebrews is regarded as Paul's, not only by the churches of the east but by all church writers who have from the beginning written in Greek."[9]

Adolph von Harnack (1851–1930), the German theologian and church historian, thought that Aquila and Priscilla wrote it jointly.[10]

The Abingdon Bible Commentary said, "Outstanding scholars as, Harnack and Rendel Harris and Peake . . . [believed] that the book was written by Priscilla with the help of her husband Aquila."[11]

My search grew more exciting. "Priscilla!" Speaking her name seemed so positive. She felt so right within me. But I could not be satisfied with this strong feeling. I needed logic, proof. I needed more than just a feeling. Why did the spirit of Priscilla dare enter my life, body, and soul when she was already mentioned in this Bible commentary?

Continuing my studies, I discovered a new covenant in The Letter to the Hebrews. When it was originally written in Greek, it used the word *suntheke*, meaning "a bond between God and the people." A bond or agreement gives us the freedom to think for ourselves. The old covenant, as written in The Letter to the Hebrews, used the Greek word *diatheke*, meaning "will."[12] The old covenant was the will of God with no freedom for us to question. But the new covenant described in Hebrews is about God's love recognizing our free will and bonding our love.

After several hours, I was tired. Libraries, I realized, did not hold the answer for which I was searching. I was painfully aware too that if scholars searching through the centuries had failed to identify the author of Hebrews, I could hope for little by the way of my amateurish attempts. I should have known, but I was so busy with my futile scratching around that my mind had been closed to the obvious source. "My God," I prayed, "if this is your will." After all, but who was I to expect anything? The moment of doubting passed. Again I was filled with a surge of strength. I knew who had written it! Priscilla! This was not the will of God but a bond between us. The new covenant was not only the will of God but also a bond made between God and his children. My initial prayer was for God's will, but no, it had to be for a bond between us.

Priscilla's message came through to me, saying, "Now is the time to step into another dimension of thinking. Instead of burdening yourself and others with your sacrifices and carrying a heavy load, you can take time to enlighten yourself by cultivating new thoughts and new knowledge."

There was much more to the message. The new covenant flowed off my pen as I read it in The Letter to the Hebrews. While humankind still has trouble adhering to the old covenant (the Ten Commandments attempting to rein in our baser nature), this new covenant was something altogether different. It spoke more to what mankind can be, what we can aspire to.

I listed the new covenant as it was unfolded to me in my reading of this precious epistle:

I.   Let love be with you (Heb. 13:1).
II.   Welcome people into your life—some might be angels (Heb. 13:2).
III.   Remember those who are suffering as though you suffered also (Heb. 13:3).
IV.   Do not be immoral (Heb. 13:4).
V.   Free yourself from greed (Heb. 13:5).
VI.   Be not afraid, for the Lord will help you (Heb. 13:6).
VII.   Remember past greatness and imitate it (Heb. 13:7).
VIII. Help one another (Heb. 13:16).
IX.   Obey your leaders and orders (Heb. 13:17).
X.   Pray (Heb. 13:18).
XI.   Have faith to believe and have confidence in someone or something that is open to question (Heb. 13:19).
XII.   Do not become discouraged; face your adversaries with respect (Heb. 13:20–21).

These new commandments were written since Christ came to us and were influenced by God's love for us.

I copied down all I possibly could of what came to me. But the most compelling part of the experience, overriding everything else, was the powerful knowledge within me, a confirmation, that Priscilla was the author of Hebrews. It was in my heart and soul. My next task was to share this with the world. I needed help.

I had to share this religious experience with someone caring and knowledgeable about the Bible. Living close to the Yale Divinity School, I naturally turned my thoughts in that direction. Who better than my friend Rev. Donald Frazier? I knew he would at least listen to me, and I was sure he would have compassion for my limitations. But it is not easy to say to anyone, however understanding, "I had a revelation about a woman writing a part of the Bible." I knew how strange it would have seemed to me if someone had told me they had a revelation. I dialed Donald and managed to convey the difficult message, revelation and all. The silence on the other end of the phone was embarrassing. He soon recovered and, being the great man and minister he was, replied, "Bring me your information or whatever you have, and I'll take a look at it."

Later in his office, I shared with him all that I could remember, the material I had written, and the tape. His advice was, "Keep it as your own personal, precious revelation . . . or do the research!"

As the days passed, I began to doubt. I questioned God, I questioned myself, and I questioned whether I had, indeed, had a revelation. I closed my mind to him and Priscilla and tried to live as though I had never heard of The Letter to the Hebrews. I am, by nature, a person who needs a great deal of freedom to be creative. How could I discipline myself to the limitations on my time and way of life that formal scholarly research would impose? It just seemed impossible. The revelation had shrunk to a hypothetical concept.

Weeks later, my insatiable curiosity and the power of the experience compelled me to go on. Reading the RSV Bible New Testament, I found where Priscilla and Aquila's names were written, with Priscilla's name mentioned first four of the six times.

- "And found a Jew named *Aquila*, a native of Pontus, who had recently come from Italy, with his wife *Priscilla*, because Claudius had commanded all Jews to leave Rome. And he went to see them;" (Acts 18:2).[13]
- "Paul stayed on in Corinth for some time. Then he left the brothers and sailed for Syria, accompanied by *Priscilla* and *Aquila*" (Acts 18:18).[14]
- "He began to speak boldly in the synagogue. When *Priscilla* and *Aquila* heard him, they invited him to their home and explained to him the way of God more adequately" (Acts 18:26).[15]

- "Greet *Priscilla* and *Aquila*, my fellow workers in Christ Jesus. They risk their lives for me. Not only I but all the churches of the Gentiles are grateful to them. Greet also the church that meets at their house" (Rom. 16:3–5).[16]
- "The churches in the province of Asia send you greetings. *Aquila* and *Priscilla* greets you warmly in the Lord, and so does the church that meets at their house" (1 Cor. 16:19).[17]
- "Greet *Priscilla* and *Aquila* and the household of Onesiphorus" (2 Tim. 4:19).[18]

It puzzled me why, in Paul's letters, this woman's name, Priscilla, was written more often first, before that of her husband, Aquila. Perhaps it was because she was of a higher social status and more educated. Reading more about her, I found that she may have come from, or may have been related to, an influential and aristocratic family. I speculated if she might have been related in some way to the early Christian Pudens family mentioned in 2 Timothy 4:21. The Pudens family was very influential, and the wife of the elder Pudens was also named Priscilla.

> *Quintus Cornelius Pudens, the elder, was one of the leading nobles of Rome and a member of the Senate. He gave shelter to Saint Peter in his house for several years, and is thought to have presented to him the curule chair, which the Apostle used as Bishop of Rome, and which is now preserved in the Vatican basilica. Till the persecution of Nero, there was no restraint on the teaching and practice of the Christian religion in Rome, except for a time under Claudius, when the tumults of the Jews made it necessary to seek safety in secrecy. It is supposed that Pudens suffered martyrdom under Nero, but we have no record of the fact. The name in the Roman Martyrology seems to be that of his son.[19]*
>
> *The wife of Quintus was named Priscilla and was quite active in helping the poor and imprisoned and caused the famous catacomb that bears her name, Saint Priscilla, on her own property near Via Salaria. Quintus C. Pudens the elder, and Priscilla had a son also called Quintus Cornelius Pudens, junior and he was also a convert and spiritual child of St. Peter.[20]*

Another resource stated that a son of Senator Quintus Cornelius Pudens was named Rufus Pudens Pudentianna and was a half-brother to the apostle Paul, thus making Priscilla Pudens their mother.[21] If that were true, could the Priscilla married to Aquila be a daughter named after her mother or even perhaps a niece?

I had discovered much later in my research that in Ruth Hoppin's book *Priscilla's Letter: Finding the Author of the Epistle to the Hebrews*, she argued that the wife of Aquila was likely a member of the Glabriones family who lived on the Pudens' property or could have been a servant or freed woman of the Cornelian or Acilian family.[22] All three of these families were related to the Pudens.

I had not known that there were two Priscillas, one married to Pudens and the other married to Aquila, but I couldn't help but feel that they were related. Having familial connections, they would have also supported each other as Christians. In Henry Spence-Jones's book *The Early Christians in Rome*, he writes the following:

> *There was also evidently a near connection between the Aquila and Priscilla so closely associated with S. Paul and the family of Pudens. It has been suggested with great probability that Aquila was a freedman or client of Pudens, and that Aquila and his wife Priscilla were intimately connected with the noble family we have been speaking of, Priscilla, S. Paul's friend, being named after the older Priscilla. All these, we know, were buried in the cemetery of Priscilla. The Priscilla who has given her name to the catacomb was the mother of Pudens.[23]*

The Pudens family's political connections extended as far as having one of their members serve as counsel and advisor to Claudius (Roman emperor, AD 41–54) and, subsequently, to Nero, until Nero went insane in AD 64. Not only did they give shelter to St. Peter for several years, but also they were able to keep the apostle Paul alive during his persecution. Ultimately, they claimed St. Paul's body after his martyrdom.

The Pudens regularly practiced Christian teachings of hospitality. Their spacious home was large enough to host worshippers and accommodate tentmakers. Priscilla and Aquila were in the trade of tent making and were living on the Pudens's property. The Pudens also welcomed guests, often prominent ones, into their household. When

Philo, a Hellenistic Jewish biblical philosopher, was invited to Rome to read his works, it is believed that he stayed with them, as did other notables. Possibly, as a result of one of these prominent guests' visits, St. Peter baptized Priscilla Pudens. Some believe that she received baptism even before Paul.

Aquila's wife, Priscilla, if not a member of a noble family, must have been connected to one. This station and connection in ancient society would have warranted her name being written before her husband's. These aristocratic connections would also explain that she was educated and had authority to interpret Jewish law.

Research and more research. Libraries became my second home. I had to close a gap of centuries by figuratively and literally digging up facts about Priscilla's family, friends, and enemies. I spent just about all my time finding out everything I could about Priscilla and the times in which she lived.

In 1978, computers and the Internet were not yet generally available, so my efforts were with index cards and dusty books. Priscilla's spirit guided me and gave me the determination and resolve that I lacked. It must have been difficult for her. I wasn't easy to convince. I was not a magician inventing a trick to pull Priscilla out of a hat. She had invaded my life. The more that I learned, the more we began to reflect each other. Our friendship developed and grew, bridging the millennia. Where once I had thought to avoid such controversy, her persistence and assurance made the effort something I looked forward to with pleasure.

Man's destruction of documents that could shed some light on her contributions and the length of time that separated us were my enemies. At various points in church history, writings that did not conform to current church doctrine were burned. People found in possession of such writings were often punished. For hundreds of years the church debated whether or not to include Hebrews as a part of the Bible. It was only at the Council of Carthage in 397 that it was finally formally included, but as a letter assumed to have been written by Paul.

As I read about this, I thought how Priscilla's teachings were first at risk from being excluded from the canon and consigned to obscurity. When The Letter to the Hebrews was finally included, it was as the work of another. Perhaps church leaders, feeling guilty for not acknowledging her authorship, granted her sainthood (which I had learned later) to helped assuage their consciences. The loss of records, either through time or design, left little information for me and others to go on.

Now having read that Aquila and Paul were tentmakers, as it stated in the book of Acts 18:2–3, I noticed tents were mentioned eight times throughout the chapter in Hebrews. As Aquila was documented as a tent maker, we can safely assume his wife would have been involved and be interested in the business in some capacity.

Examples from the Bible:

- "a minister in the sanctuary, and the true *tent* [tabernacle] which is set up [pitched] not by man but by the Lord" (Heb. 8:2).[24]
- "For a *tent* [tabernacle] was prepared [it continues with her feminine descriptions of the furnishings in the tent]" (Heb. 9:2).[25]
- "These preparations having thus been made, the priests go continually into the outer *tent*, performing their ritual duties" (Heb. 9:6).[26]
- "By this the Holy Spirit indicates that the way into the sanctuary is not yet opened as long as the outer *tent* is still standing (which is symbolic for the present age)" (Heb. 9:8–9).[27] (See Exodus 26:31–33.)
- "But when Christ appeared as a high priest of the good things that have come then through the greater and more perfect *tent* (not made by hands, that is, not of this creation)" (Heb. 9:11).[28]
- "And in the same way he sprinkled with the blood both *tent* and all the vessels used in worship" (Heb. 9:21).[29]
- "By faith he sojourned in the land of promise, as in a foreign land, living in *tents* with Isaac and Jacob, heirs with him of the same promise" (Heb. 11:9).[30]
- "We have an altar from which those who serve the *tent* [tabernacle] have no right to eat" (Heb. 13:10).[31]

There is more evidence that Hebrews was written by a woman. It has 6,900 words, and it is the third longest epistle of the thirteen written in the New Testament, yet there is an apology in it for its brevity! Hebrews 13:22 states the following:

I appeal to you brethren, bear with my word of exhortation, for I have written to you briefly.[32]

Another translation for it is as follows:

> *And I beseech you, brethren; suffer the word of exhortation, for*
> *I have written a letter unto you in few words.*[33]

Women are more likely to use apologies as a way to establish peer relationships. Certainly a man with the education and talent to create a work such as The Letter to the Hebrews would not be one to easily and needlessly apologize. Yet Priscilla was not trying to apologize for the briefness of her letter by comparing it with other letters. Rather, her apology was for having to condense her great message. She was seeking to remind the reader of their religious heritage and to give them the principles for fulfilling their faith.

Something kept bringing my eyes back to the eleventh chapter. I could see there were several messages there. In an effort to condense The Letter, she suggested that the recipients refer to their Old Testament. She said the following in Hebrews 11:32:

> *And what more shall I say? For time would fail me to tell of*
> *Gideon, Barak, Samson, Jephthah, of David and Samuel, and*
> *the prophets . . .*[34]

In today's language, she would be saying, "You look it up! I do not have the time to write every detail. You read about your ancestors, while I write to you about your new faith. Here is an important message, commandments for you to live your faith by. People are dying for this faith, and I have to write this to you as briefly as possible. It deserves more than my brief words."

Next, I wondered why Priscilla referred to these six men from the Old Testament. What bond did they share? Throughout history, scholars have wondered what these men had in common for their names to be grouped together.

She goes on to say the following in Hebrews 11:33–34:

> *who, through faith, conquered kingdoms, enforced justice,*
> *received promises, stopped the mouths of lions, quenched raging*
> *fire, escaped the edge of the sword, won strength out of weakness,*
> *became mighty in war, put foreign armies to flight.*[35]

Reading the story of each of these men who lived in different times in history, I could see their similarity. Evidently, this was the reason Priscilla referred to them:

Gideon, the least of his family, the weakest son, became a leader of his people (Judg. 6–7).

Barak listened to Deborah and helped her win battles, even when she told him, "If you follow me, the honor of conquering will go to a woman instead of you" (Judg. 4–5).

Samson was always fighting alone. He was strong but was defeated and blinded because of a woman, Delilah, but regained his strength (Judg. 13–16).

Jephthah was the son of a harlot, whose father's wife tossed him out of his house. Later, his vow to God cost him the life of his daughter. He was driven to be an outlaw but then was called by his people and won tremendous battles (Judg. 11–12).

David was a mere shepherd boy who became king. He listened to his wife, Bathsheba, and gave her the wish of having her son as king (1 Kings 1:11–30).

Samuel was born late to his mother, Hannah, who, in her gratefulness to the Lord, gave her son at the age of three to the priest to do the Lord's work. He became strong and faithful to God, even among the rebellious people (1 Sam. 1:1–28).

What did these men have in common? Each started from weakness and grew strong. Most were influenced in his belief by the greater strength and courage of a woman and were not afraid to stand for their beliefs! Priscilla's letter was to encourage its recipients to have the courage of their ancestors to pursue their faith.

Another passage gave me more evidence that it was a woman writing. It has a description of the temple where Jews worshipped. But there is a difference between the description in Exodus (Old Testament) and that in The Letter to the Hebrews (New Testament). This is what she wrote in The Letter to the Hebrews 9:2–5:

> *For a tent was prepared, the outer one in which were the lamp-stand and the table and the bread of the Presence; it is called the Holy Place.* Behind *the second curtain stood a tent called the Holy of Holies, having the golden altar of incense and the ark*

*of the covenant covered on all sides with gold, which contained
a golden urn holding the manna, and Aaron's rod that budded,
and the tables of the covenant, above it were the cherubim of
glory over-shadowing the mercy seat. Of these things we cannot
now speak in detail.*[36]

But some of these things, which the author described, as in the Holy
of Holies, were actually placed in front of the curtain in the tent, not
inside. Examples are as follows:

- "You shall set the altar of burnt offerings *before the door* of the
  tabernacle of the tent of the meeting" (Exod. 40:6).[37]
- "And he put the table in the tent of meeting, on the north side
  of the Tabernacle, *outside the veil*" (Exod. 40:22).[38]
- "And he put the golden altar in the tent of meeting *before the
  veil*" (Exod. 40:26).[39]

The author could not speak in detail because women in those days
were not permitted to view the Holy of Holies. A male author would
have known where the furnishings were placed in the Holy of Holies,
or the Holy Place. He would not have bothered with descriptions of
furnishings, as a woman would, especially in this brief letter.

This research would have been difficult for me if it had not been
for frequent encouragement along the way. My experience the morning
after a big Connecticut snowstorm in February 1978 was typical of the
unseen force leading me along. I had an appointment with Sister Francis
DeSales Hefferman, president of Albertus Magnus College, followed by
another with Rev. John Irvine, president of the Lay School of Religion
at Yale. They were to read and hear about my religious experience.

But the storm had closed the college, and cars were not moving. I
did not want to miss the appointments, so I decided to walk. The world
around me seemed to be sleeping under a deep blanket of snow. The air
was cold and the walking a challenge, but I felt no concern. The hot
cup of coffee, which Sister Francis served me at her convent, was very
welcome. She listened attentively as I told my story. I was eager to know
what a woman of her stature and religious education thought. She spoke
very positively about the revelation, the research I was doing, and urged
me to continue. She was very encouraging, and I enjoyed being with her.

Before leaving her study, I remembered that I had brought with me a book, *The Genesee Diary*, which I had promised to give to Sister Thoma, a fellow artist and teacher and a resident of the convent. As Sister Francis reached for the book, promising to deliver it, she looked past me toward the window and laughed, for there at that moment, trudging by in the deep snow, was Sister Thoma. Sister Francis brought her in, and we shared a laugh over the perfect timing.

Our conference ended on a happy note, and I left wondering why I was not more concerned about the impossibility of keeping my next appointment, a two-mile walk through unshoveled snow. A beautiful silence filled the air in the white fairyland. It was a strange sight to see abandoned cars under mounds of snow. Was I the only foolhardy person to be walking in the street?

The rattling of snow tire chains from a lone mail truck broke the quiet. It stopped, and the driver asked if I needed a ride! Could a mail truck pick up a passenger? I don't think the US Postal Service would approve! I could hardly believe it, and I thought it might be against the rules, but I was enjoying the mysterious force leading me on. I asked myself why I didn't admit that it was God leading me. Was it because I had yet to fully submit to him, or did I find myself feeling unworthy to serve him? I accepted the ride and balanced myself as I stood in the truck while we drove to my next destination, Rev. John Irvine's office. *Had John been able to get through the snow to his office and keep the appointment?* I wondered.

The Harkness Tower's chimes from Yale University were playing their twelve o'clock music as I entered his office. I was feeling a bit like Cinderella—a little corny, I know, but true. The whole experience made me feel light-headed and amazed. Surprisingly, John was there and seemed to know the mailman who picked me up. John and I had lunch together while he listened to the tape of my Priscilla revelation. He found it fascinating. Afterward he asked if I would consider teaching the same course, the Spirituality of Religion in Art, in the fall semester at Yale Divinity, Lay School of Religion. Everything was so positive. "Yes, of course, I would."

Several weeks later, after a discussion one evening with some Divinity students, Carol Berry, my art assistant, and I went to her apartment to read some books she borrowed for me from the Divinity School Library. We found an article by M. J. Shroyer in the *Interpreters'*

Dictionary of the Bible, published by Abingdon Press. Shroyer was a noted scholar who wrote about Priscilla, saying, "She is named first in the instruction of Apollos as she was more capable than her husband . . . Various authorities have nominated her the author of The Letter to the Hebrews."

As for Carol and I, we were both ecstatic over finding this article by Shroyer and in knowing that someone else believed as we did. My finger was still on this article in the book when Carol's phone rang. It was a student who, earlier that evening, had heard my story about Priscilla. She had called to say that she had just been told that today, February 13, was the feast day of St. Priscilla in the Eastern church.

We had not known until just then that Priscilla was a saint! What did this mean? Was it a sign to give us added encouragement to pursue this further? It seemed an incredible coincidence! We wondered if this was what it meant to walk with God. Could this be a two-thousand-year-old valentine to all women from Priscilla? Was she saying "I love you" on Valentine's Eve? Romantic and beautiful, I know, but this is the message of her letter: the bonding of celestial love with earthly love. The phenomena of the timing in all these experiences were a constant wonderment to me.

Late that night, I wrote a letter to Henri Nouwen in Rome. While he was at Yale, I had attended his vespers and Mass in the cellar of the Divinity school's tower. My husband and I had opened our home to Henri and his friends until he had left to teach in Rome. I wrote to him, telling him about the exciting experience I was having with a two-thousand-year-old woman and my belief that she wrote a part of the Bible. Then I waited anxiously for his response.

CHAPTER FOUR

A Needed Break . . .
Then More Discoveries

In the following weeks, my husband, my youngest daughter, Amy, and I were invited to spend a winter vacation with our daughter Dana and her husband at their home in Puerto Rico. It was what I needed, a place with sunshine and no snow. It was a delightful vacation. Taking this much-needed break, I thought I had left the spirit of Priscilla behind.

We visited many little towns on the island and enjoyed being with our children in their tropical home. We were also pleasantly surprised to be invited as special guests of Harold Craft, the director at Cornell's Arecibo Observatory, to view the world's largest radio telescope. We drove many twisting miles high into the mountains, dodging chickens and seeing broken-down cars on the side of the road.

Carolyn in Arecibo

We finally arrived at a high fence that was guarded by a man carrying a rifle. He checked us in and called ahead before he opened the gates. I was surprised to see that this telescope was in the shape of a huge saucer, larger than a football field and nestled between the rising rock karsts. Director Craft told us that, at the time, the telescope was examining a pulsar born from a collapsed star in the constellation of Aquila. Shaking my head and smiling to myself, I thought, *Even here in Puerto Rico, Priscilla and her husband, Aquila, followed me.*

I asked permission to walk under the edges of the saucer but was told to stay only a short time since the telescope's operation sometimes left faint traces of radioactivity. I was able to see small holes in the steel sheets that made up the saucer, enabling sunlight to filter through to the lush growths of numerous green ferns. They reminded me of how some of the earth's first plants were ferns and were subjected to radioactivity, as were these.

In the director's office, I saw a drawing of Leonardo da Vinci's *Vitruvian Man* on their instruments. This image was being transmitted into space as evidence of man's presence on Earth. Hearing about the pulsars in the constellation of Aquila and the transmission of this image into space made a lasting impression on me. Was my trip divinely planned? As I looked at the observatory star charts, I thought they were far beyond my limited capability to ever understand. I could not have dreamed how important this trip would prove for Priscilla and me.

We spent many more days of enjoyment at my daughter's home, lazily swinging in hammocks at the beach and watching migrating whales spout. While lying on the beach one day, something wonderful and unexpected happened to me. My family was swimming and snorkeling, and I was settling down to sunbathe. I pulled my straw hat over my face, listening to the sound of the surf crashing on the coral reefs and feeling the whispers of the wind through the slits of my hat. A beautiful peace was settling upon me.

Suddenly, a consuming force took over my body, and I felt a glorious exultation. It wasn't the same kind of energy as my earlier revelation. It was all the feelings of happiness from across the span of my life drawing back into me in a single magnificent moment. A total joyous embrace. A taste of heaven. I wanted to stay and linger in that moment, but I felt it was not time to keep it, and I had some power to let it go. It was frightening and exalting. I immediately wondered what button I could press so I could recapture it later, but it was gone. It was the most magnificent wholeness of feelings. "Thank you, God!"

I wanted to shout out my experience, but it seemed too precious to put into words and have others try to analyze it. Does describing the mechanics of a kiss tell you what a kiss is? The very telling can destroy a precious moment. Even writing it now seems to belittle this special personal spiritual experience.

Priscilla had followed me to Puerto Rico in spite of my efforts to take a break and leave her behind. I had learned about stars and pulsars in the constellation with the same name as her husband. And I had most definitely received a blessing. Science, history, religion, and blessings, all mixing together. Looking back, it's clear that this was preparing me for journeys that I had no idea were ahead.

In the stack of mail I found waiting for me upon our arrival at home was a letter from Henri Nouwen. Beautiful Vatican stamps adorned the envelope. It was his reply to a letter I had sent him about my Priscilla revelation. He encouraged me. He stated his doubts about a woman writing a part of the Bible, but he also hoped that I might be right. It would make the Bible so complete. This was what I needed: constructive doubt. Henri wrote, "The author of The Letter to the Hebrews was someone of Jewish, Christian, and Hellenistic background, was a friend of Paul, and lived in Rome."

How did Priscilla qualify? I already knew these things and that Priscilla met all those criteria, except that I was unsure about *Hellenistic*. Where could I possibly find out about that, especially since I wasn't even certain what the word *Hellenistic* meant?

That very night, my husband read an article on Vincent van Gogh in *The People's Almanac* by Wallenchinsky and Wallace. The article was of interest to him because he knew that Henri had taught a course on van Gogh at Yale Divinity School. When he turned to the last page of the article in this very large book, there on the opposite page was another article titled "She Wrote It, He Got the Credit."[40] He woke me up to confront me with this strange coincidence.

My eyes were barely open as we read the article that mentioned a book by Ruth Hoppin called *Author of the Epistle to the Hebrews*. This was my first introduction to her work. In it she wrote that the apostle Paul received credit for writing The Letter to the Hebrews and that she believed the author was really Priscilla. How good it felt to not be alone in this research and belief.

It thrilled me to find this affirmation. Yet I also felt a mixture of sadness too as I thought I was the only one to be given the message about her authorship. I wanted to be special. It took me a while to realize that the Lord would not have chosen just one person to reveal this truth. If he had twelve disciples in the beginning, he must have had many more disciples to continue his work across the centuries. He has more today, and there will be many more yet to come. Christianity is not history but a continuing living experience, forever moving forward. It is a *living* Bible.

When my friend and assistant, Carol, heard about this book, she asked her husband, Steve, to find it at the Divinity School Library. He did not know how to respond to her request, for he had already secretly purchased it to surprise her on her birthday! When her birthday arrived, before she had even read it, and in her always-gracious manner, she offered to loan it to me. Eagerly reading it right away, I found that although Ruth Hoppin took different avenues investigating Priscilla's authorship, her book reaffirmed my research.

In April, I started another religion in art course for the Church of the Redeemer. Though it was spring and nature was repeating its newness, I felt caught in a rut. Having to do this class again seemed so complicated and burdensome. I would have to include both religious philosophy and painting techniques while at the same time accommodating beginners and advanced students. How could I interest one group without boring the other and have everyone complete a satisfactory painting? All in a two-hour period! What I really wanted to do was to speak about and concentrate on Priscilla. I knelt to pray for God's guidance and asked him to continue to use me and to take me into the next phase of my Priscilla discoveries. I gathered my easel and bag and headed for the door. As I opened the front door to leave, I suddenly came face-to-face with the mailman. He handed me a package, some junk mail, and a colorful postcard from Henri encouraging me in the pursuit of Priscilla. The timing was perfect.

My first class was to be about the importance of nothing. The focus was the importance of leaving space around the subject of a painting. We must leave a space for the halos. Once again I thought of how Henri spoke of the importance of emptiness, leaving a space so God could enter in. My mind became filled with the importance of the nothing. I thought about our finite minds, how difficult it is for us to relate to God, who is infinite. He is beyond our complete comprehension, unexplainable, a mystery.

Before greeting my students that morning, I thought how ironic it was that we might be worshipping and loving a void. Someday everything will be gone. We will have *nothing* left but God, and we will embrace this void and call it Father. If we love a void, then the *nothing* is *more* valuable than a tangible *something*. There cannot be something without the nothing giving space for its existence (even today, quantum physics has discovered this). I wanted to swing around and embrace the air.

I got silly over the whole concept and carried the thought a step further. God must truly love us, for look at the shape we are in when he takes us! I opened the door to the classroom and announced to the class, "We are no bargain!" Then I gave them their assignment. We would study Oriental paintings and the respect they have for the subject, leaving space around it. This is in contrast to our Western style, in which we tend to crowd our paintings as we crowd our lives.

In mid-April, my students and I went on a field trip to New York to see the American Watercolor Society show. We stopped first for lunch at the Metropolitan Museum of Art. Afterward, we wandered around its bookstore, where I selected a book from a high shelf called *The Art of the Copts*.[41] As I opened it, the book seemed to automatically open to page 85. The logical explanation was that this was where the binding was sewn. Yet on that very page, in the upper right-hand corner, was a drawing of a statue of Isis in the Louvre. The description said that the statue had been discovered in Priscilla's catacomb (a Priscilla catacomb! I had no idea!). Here was a tie between Priscilla and the Hellenistic (ancient Greek) culture. The Greco-Roman empires had adopted many deities from the Egyptians, and Isis was one image that eventually evolved toward Christianity's Madonna. Henri Nouwen had said that the author of The Letter to the Hebrews must have been a Jew, then a Christian, a friend of Paul, have lived in Rome, and have had Hellenistic ties. I had already known that Priscilla met most of these criteria, and now the last one had fallen into place. I purchased the book, copied that page, and sent it to Henri at the Pontifical Gregorian University in Rome.

The idea that there was a Priscilla catacomb intrigued me. I had to see it. I needed to go there! I didn't know, or even have a feeling, that I would find any new information. I just needed to be near where she once existed. As a scholar of the Civil War needs to go to Gettysburg after they have studied generals and battles, I needed to go to her catacomb.

Was this just another coincidence? How much does God have to hit me over the head to convince me of his astute timing? I realized I had an important contact in Rome. I reached out to my friend Henri in a letter, asking what I should do. I waited anxiously for his response. Was he just going to try to placate this woman who had a religious experience, or was he going to spell it out loud and clear as one honest friend to another? His greatness showed through again. He was a true, great priest. A priest who is a bridge bringing people to God. He wrote, "Come to Rome!" He said he was inspired by my new findings about Priscilla. He arranged an English-speaking guide for me in Rome and asked me to send him the address of the catacombs.

Joy, pure joy, followed me all day. I was now certain Priscilla was saying, "It is not I who is important. It is the message I bring to all people. Here is the chain that connects the old with the new. Here is your heritage, the roots from which you grow, here in my letter to the Hebrews."

If I were to go to Rome—was I going to Rome? I was going to Rome! Unfortunately, there was a stumbling block. I needed a letter of recommendation to visit the Priscilla catacomb. I telephoned the Hartford Archdiocese to ask for the letter. The archbishop's secretary said that they would first need to know the accredited organization that was sponsoring my research. Then they would have to receive approval from the university I represented, and with that approval, the diocese would write Rome to get their approval, which in turn would write to the State because both the church and State had to approve.

Then the secretary said, "And you expect all this within three weeks?"

I replied in a small voice, "Yes."

With that, he asked if I had anything else I wanted to say. How could I respond, knowing the impatience on the other end of the line? I did not have the right words or answers to satisfy him. And of course, I didn't represent any university.

This wasn't good. How was I to penetrate one of the world's oldest and largest bureaucracies without any credentials? It would have been hard enough if I were a Yale-sponsored PhD.

I found out through friends that the archbishop of Hartford had written his thesis on the Dead Sea Scrolls. The first person to recognize the Dead Sea Scrolls for what they were was Mar Athanasius Yeshua Samuel, a metropolitan of the Syrian Jacobite Monastery of St. Mark in Jerusalem. Known as Metropolitan Sam, he had great difficulty convincing many scholarly authorities that the scrolls were genuine and was repeatedly disappointed when they did not believe him.[42]

Samuel and I had the same problem. It would be impossible to convey my entire three months of experience in a single letter or phone conversation with the archbishop's secretary. I wrote the archbishop a letter mentioning Metropolitan Sam and my hope that he would give me the needed referrals. I could now truly relate to Priscilla's challenge: trying to convey her important message in a single letter.

Several days later, I received an acknowledgment of my letter from the archbishop's secretary. That was all. Shouldn't I have some credentials to show in Rome? But they gave me nothing. All I had was this acknowledgment letter. Well, this will have to do. I knew the time was right, so I booked my flight on Trans World Airlines for May 14.

On the morning of May 1, I had an appointment with Dean Colin W. Williams at the Yale Divinity School. I thought he was most gracious to be listening to me, and as I started to explain my research, I wondered if I was saying the right things. But he mentioned Priscilla's name before I did! He said his father had told him that if any woman had a part in writing the Bible, he believed it would have been Priscilla. Dean Williams encouraged me, asked if he could read my manuscript (which I hadn't even started yet!), and invited me to come back after my trip to Italy.

Henri sent me catalogues of information about the Priscilla catacomb. I studied the maps of the many subterranean paths and loges. This trip was going to be nerve-racking and exciting at the same time. I had never traveled outside the United States before, and certainly not alone! As I was going over all the arrangements with my family, a friend who had lived in Rome stopped over. She gave me a gettone coin to drop into the Italian telephone and a number to call as she skeptically remarked, "Just as a precaution in case the priest doesn't show up at the airport."

In the days before my trip, newspaper headlines were not encouraging:

May 9:   "Kidnapped Moro Found Slain Today in Rome: 55 Days after His Kidnapping by Red Brigades"

May 10:   "Italy Activates Alert to Quell Terrorists: Police Impose Emergency Plan"

May 12:   "Terrorist Wound Official in Milan: Shooting of Christian Democrats and Business Executives in the Knees"

We have friends in Italy who are Christian Democrats. They were the host parents for our daughter Dana, who was an American Field Service exchange student in 1971. I was worried for them and decided I would try to get in touch with them while I was there to offer my support.

Where did this tremendous drive come from that was taking me far away from my home? It was an awesome and wondrous feeling. Yet at the same time, I did not have a single doubt about going to Rome. If God had led me this far, then he was sending me on a mission and would take care of me.

He had given me inspiration, and he had revealed things to me in sequence. He had shown me the way at every step. He had brought a Catholic priest into my life to help me on my spiritual journey and to show me the way to Priscilla's catacomb. There was a pattern to the mission. I prayed I could abide by the bond of the Spirit guiding me.

CHAPTER FIVE

My Diary in Rome, 1978

May 14

A storm prevented takeoffs and landings at JFK. My exciting journey started with a four-hour delay and lots of rain. As I was seated in the limousine before I left home for the airport and as the luggage was being loaded, someone tapped on my window. I rolled down the foggy window and was surprised to find Dr. Robert Kendall, a good friend, grinning at me. He handed me some dripping-wet letters to deliver when I got to Rome. This was an exciting setting for the beginning of an adventure. I was worried, though, and hoped someone would be there to meet me at the other end even after this long delay. I had no hotel reservations and spoke not a word of Italian. This certainly was going to be a journey of faith.

The day before, Henri's secretary, Jane Bouvier, had given me a copy of his book *The Genesee Diary*, newly published in German. She also gave me copies of the latest magazine articles about him. I was to deliver all these to him in Rome. I reassured myself with the thought that I didn't need to be too concerned about being met. Everything felt so positive. The Lord was with me, especially since I had Henri's papers to deliver!

May 15

I arrived and passed through customs at Leonardo da Vinci Airport with hundreds of others from the 747. There in the crowd outside of customs was a young man holding up a sign with my name on it. What a fun and thrilling surprise to see my name in a foreign country. And there was something comforting about it too. He handed me a note, which said the following:

Dear Carolyn,

> *Welcome to Rome. This is Giorgo; he will take you to a convent. Do not pay him. I will call you this evening.*
>
> *Henri*

I was exhausted but excited. I was going to be staying in a convent. What a surprise! Giorgo and I arrived at the Convent of the Resurrection in the heart of Rome. The street front of the convent was a large wall with heavy double doors. We were met by a small nun in a black habit. She guided me into another world, one of serenity and quiet, apart from the busy street. The convent took up a city block and stood five stories high. It had a school, courtyard, and chapel on the ground floor. With high ceilings and white marble floors, it was a cool and inviting oasis. Giorgo left, and a sweet American sister named Wanda showed me to my room. We climbed to the fourth floor, walked down a long corridor, crossed an open terrace, and entered another lengthy marble corridor.

Once we arrived at my room, Sister Wanda instructed me on the rules of the house. When leaving my room, I was to lock my door and hang the key on a hook within full view so that the maid could unlock the door to clean.

"Why should I bother to lock it?" I asked.

She looked surprised. "Why? So that no one will enter while you're gone."

Every time I hung the key on the hook, I continued to wonder why, but when in Rome . . .

My room was approximately twelve feet by fourteen feet, with marble flooring and French windows overlooking the beautiful courtyard. Just beyond the rooftop, I could see the dome of St. Peter's. Over my bed was a wooden crucifix. The other furnishings in the room included a desk, a bookcase, an armoire, and a bed table with lamp. The bathroom was next door. This was to be my home in Rome.

A delicious meal waited in the dining room—veal chops, german fried potatoes, stuffed tomatoes, chicken broth, hot home-baked biscuits, and raspberry gelatin pie. It was a special feast day. The sisters from many different orders, with and without habits, were beautiful and delightful to be with. They were from various parts of the world and had come to Rome for renewal. Two of them had escaped from the massacre in Somalia and were waiting to return. These two were so thin.

After our dinner, we visited the garden, where there were roses, calla lilies, and like a Monet painting, a fountain with large goldfishes and a few white marble statues. Heavenly music filled the garden. I heard an organ playing in the chapel and nuns singing. All my senses were affected. My sense of taste, smell, and now my ears were being pleased. Sister Wanda invited me to attend chapel. Inside, there were enough colorful flowers to delight any artist. They accented and contrasted with the nuns in their black habits. How refreshing and good it felt to give thanks to the Lord!

Later, Sister Charles Marie tapped on my door to say hello and to tell me of my appointment with Henri for that evening. She was the librarian for the Pontifical Gregorian University. She had helped Henri find this place for me to stay.

Sometime after 9:00 p.m., Sister Juanita, from Australia, and Sister Zita, from Africa, took me to Henri's apartment on top of Janiculum Hill (Gianicolo in Italian), overlooking all of Rome. I thought, *He must feel like a Roman emperor!* He looked wonderful and was most gracious to us. I was very tired, and we visited only a short time. We shared wine, and I met Daniel Sanders, who would be my guide the next day. Daniel was a cheerful man who was to be ordained in Milwaukee, Wisconsin, in a few months. I was told that I would visit the catacombs the next day, and for the day after that, Henri had arranged an audience with the pope!

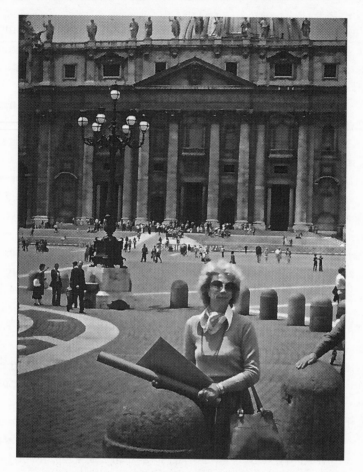

Carolyn at the Piazzo San Pietro, Roma, Italy

May 16

It was a beautiful sunny day, and I could hear the bustle of the morning traffic as I wrote in my diary. I should have been dressing as it was getting late, and I had to go to the Vatican Bank that morning. As I returned from my morning bath in a huge old tub, I found on my bedside table a tray with a thermos of coffee, thick slices of raisin bread, some cheese, and an orange. How very thoughtful someone was. It was such a beautiful day, and I had so much to look forward to. I had to begin.

11:30 a.m.—My first excursion was to the Vatican Bank with Sister Zita. I received a better exchange rate for my money there than I would have outside in the city of Rome. I also appreciated the smaller denominations and precious coins. I became very highly aware of Roman Catholic power vibrating in the air. I had never seen so many people of religious orders. I had mixed feelings about the sheer magnitude of devotion. I resolved to think this through at some future time. I was now on my own and decided to try my wings surviving in spite of my language barrier. I stopped at a card shop in St. Peter's, followed an American tour group, and then wandered off alone. I enjoyed the art and visiting the Papal Historical Museum before catching the bus for the convent and lunch. At the convent, I freshened up and changed my clothes, and I was off to meet Dan Sanders, my guide for the day.

Sister Maria Francesca took us down into the depths of our first stop, the oldest of catacombs, Priscilla's. I was overcome with emotion on arriving at the place I had only dreamed of seeing. Priscilla had become so much a part of my life that I trembled at the sight of the ancient dust suspended and floating in the guide's flashlight beam as it searched the walls and ceilings of her tomb. The catacomb was first a Jewish one, as depicted by the paintings. As Christianity grew from Judaism, it became a Christian catacomb. This made it the oldest Christian catacomb in Rome. I thought I would be frightened in those deep caverns, but I felt very comfortable.

I could have spent hours there. But the rules and strict nuns prevented it. There was also a rule against picture taking, but this was not a tourist trip—this was research! I had to disobey. I snapped some photos, and then my camera jammed! During the tour, I would, at times, deviate from the path, using my own flashlight to explore a little of the other unvisited tunnels. This would be hardly worth mentioning, except that Daniel Sanders admonished me for disobeying the rules. He observed that my new camera had jammed moments later and alluded to it being a fitting punishment.

My every sense was attuned to the moment. I listened intently to what was being said by our guide, but I was also listening to the past. My eyes darted up and down, left and right. Why am I here? Where do I look? What am I overlooking? What am I seeing that I cannot perceive? The paintings on the walls were primitive scenes: a shepherd with sheep; paintings of people with their arms over their heads, some wearing strange costumes; paintings of birds and other frescos showing people poised in action. But I couldn't understand what they were saying. Why were these primitive paintings in a dark, deep, dank, dimly lit catacomb? My thoughts were often interrupted by the need to look down at the moist, slippery paths of mud we had to follow. I felt that the guide's narration was only part of the truth that was down here. How could I know that? What great force had taken me to this place?

Suddenly I was blind! I could not see the path, the niches where the bodies were held, or anything else. There was only complete blackness. I rubbed my eyes to see if they were open or closed. My eyelashes were fluttering open, but I saw nothing. To reach this high point in my mission only to suddenly go blind was intensely frightening and frustrating. Sister Maria Francesca's voice came through the void and explained that the meter for the lights had expired. We were to stay still until she added more coins and returned. Exhaling a deep relieved breath, I pressed the switch on my flashlight.

As we continued down the path, I noticed that most of the niches for the bodies, called loculi, were very small and mostly empty. The people who lived in those days must have been smaller than we are today. It would be very easy to become lost down here. I remember reading that there were six hundred miles of catacombs. The ceiling was about twelve feet high and the paths four feet wide. About every thirty feet, a lone low-watt lightbulb dangled from an electrical wire. This would never have been permitted if open to the public in the United States. Also, we would have glamorized this ancient site. But here in Italy, it was as history had left it.

Clearly, sometime in the past, it had been looted. I gave thanks that I had been allowed to witness and touch the stones that Priscilla and Peter had once touched. Down here, under her home, in the catacombs was a two-thousand-year-old Greek chapel (*capella Greca*) ransacked and in ruins, with only ancient crude and cracked and chipped frescoes remaining with broken tombs. Yet I grew excited in the knowledge that Priscilla had a Greek chapel! This was another proof of her Hellenistic background. Deep down inside me, I wanted to shout her name, "Priscilla!" I felt she could hear me.

I learned that the catacombs had been sealed for hundreds of years because of a plague. Then Antonio Bosio, a monk, opened them in1593.[43] *Roma Sotterranea*, his works, and his drawings were published in 1632 by the Order of Malta. The catacombs had been resealed and had been opened again by Christian archaeologists, such as Monsignor Bottari (1734–1754) and Giovanni Battista de Rossi (1822–1894).[44]

As we continued our visit, I saw a graffito of Bosio's signature on a wall and also the archaeologist Carrara's name with the date 1777. I had read their fascinating and informative writings about this catacomb and the reports by de Rossi of the secrets buried there. There were miles of galleries (corridors) with loculi, going down for many levels, all carved out from the lava rock that lay beneath and supported Rome. My flashlight beamed through decades of suspended dust onto ancient frescoes. I caught sight of a large stone with the inscription Priscilla C. The *C* signified Clarissima, which means "of Senatorial rank."[45] With this title, Priscilla would have had influence. Combined with her probable familial connection to the consul Acili Glabriones,[46] she would have had sufficient influence to ensure that Paul's first troubles in Italy resulted only in house arrest and not imprisonment (Acts 28:16). I believe Priscilla's body had been in a large niche in a particular wall near some stairs, but the nun who guided us did not speak of this as we passed. As I raised my flashlight, it illuminated this ancient second-century wall. There on the wall was a painting of Priscilla dressed in a purple senatorial robe and wearing a rabbi's shawl. The Bible describes Priscilla as a teacher. The fresco showed her to be an early rabbi or priest.

Priscilla in rabbinic shawl

Another fresco caught my eye. It appeared to be a double painting on the catacomb's ceiling. This double painting was of the Madonna and child and a man standing next to them, pointing over her head to another painting. The pointing man in the fresco was explained to me to be a prophet. The second painting was perpendicular to the first and depicted a shepherd with sheep standing beneath two fruit trees. I was able to take several pictures of these to study later as my camera seemed to be working again.

We came up from the catacombs long before I was ready. Dan and I took a taxi to St. Pudentia's Church. Unfortunately, the excavated remains of the Pudens's house under the church were flooded, and we were unable to visit. Over a cup of cappuccino and some pastry, I told Daniel about what I had learned of Priscilla and the purpose of my visit to Rome. I knew I talked too much, but he was a generous listener. We joked about the camera that was now working. He suggested we visit the nearby Church of St. Prassede. This lifted my spirits for this saint was a descendent of Priscilla, and I felt it was a good thing to do. I tried to keep myself relaxed so that I could do the Lord's bidding and not my own. It was as if I were living a prayer.

We found this church such fun to explore. I pointed to the fine trompe l'oeil paintings. We tried to separate painted shadows from real shadows, real frames from paintings of frames, and a painted column from the ancient real one next to it. We enjoyed being fooled and discovering the real among the unreal.

In the oldest part of the church was an oratory with a magnificent mosaic. I took a picture of it, explaining to Dan about the square halo on only one of the women in the portrait of four women. Square halos were only depicted on living saints and were very rare.[47] I hoped I could have a square halo someday. See photo image on page 62)

At 7:00 p.m., we each hurried off to have supper at our respective homes. I had found this handsome young man such a gentle and pleasant person to be with. I hoped he had found some pleasure in this day also. Dinner then a bath. I tried to prepare for the papal audience scheduled for the next day. Sister Charles Marie came to my room and presented me with a bottle of wine. We toasted the day. There was so much to do in Rome. I had no time to write home, though I had mailed a small postcard to my husband, Dan, from the Vatican that morning. I resolved to find time to call the people I was supposed to contact in Rome. To quote Priscilla's letter, "but time is too brief" for me to tell them. Good night, sweet world. Thank you.

May 17

The day of my wedding anniversary. I felt homesick and thought of my husband, Daniel, and my life with him at home. I had a light breakfast at seven forty-five and received a call from Henri, telling me how and when to be at the audience with the pope. Henri also gave me directions to the chapel at the Pontifical North American College, where he would be officiating afterward. This I was anxious to witness.

Pope Paul VI was twenty-five minutes late for the audience, so I was only able to stay a short time before leaving to see Henri. The pope had two men help him climb a few stairs to his chair (Pope Paul VI died about a month later). I listened to him (the interpretation), received a blessing, and then ran all the way to the Pontifical North American College. Henri's Mass was very impressive. It involved twelve priests and several hundred young seminarians.

The chapel was beautiful, with modern expressionistic paintings on the walls—huge murals. They were so large that I felt I was inside them as they surrounded me. The floor was dark-green marble with curves of white, resembling the sea and foam. Henri had arranged for a seminarian to sit with me, though I did not realize it at the time, and I would not give up my seat at the end of the pew to him. Sitting on my other side, he explained that he was there to answer any questions I might have.

As the Mass started, Henri and the twelve priests formally processed down the aisle. As he passed, he turned toward me and gestured for me to sit farther up, closer to the altar. Such a wonderful man, more concerned about helping others even in the midst of his religious duties. I wanted to receive communion from him, but there was no more wine when I reached his chalice. Our encounters always seem to create the unusual. I wondered what would happen next. He very gracefully guided me across the front of the altar to receive communion from another priest.

The music was exceptionally beautiful and contemporary, composed by a young seminarian from Providence, Rhode Island. There was an organ, piano, violin, and guitar along with the strong, rich voices of the men. The music had an exquisite rhythm that made my whole being want to react. I wanted to stay in this newfound heaven. That was an hour of my life I would cherish and wish I could live again. Its memory still lingers on and on.

After Mass, dinner at the college was attended by hundreds of young men. Before everyone was seated, someone announced to the whole room over a loudspeaker that I was a guest of Henri's. I missed the details, but everyone applauded. I was embarrassed and numb but flattered. Dan Sanders came to the table to welcome me. I don't remember what we had to eat, but the dessert was an artist's creation of St. Peter's dome made from strawberry shortcake!

Afterward, I felt the need to take a very long walk. This day was all so very magnificent but confusing. Yes, confusing. What did it all mean? I thought back to the seminary and of our social and religious customs going against natural norms. All those wonderful young seminarians choosing spirituality service and worship over family life and the world outside. I was tired and perplexed that I should feel this way. It had been such an exhilarating day. This thought ran through my mind, "When you hear that different drummer, just be aware of the effect the sound has on others, then go your own way, with thanksgiving for this day."

Back at the convent, Sister Charles brought me some hand cream for my dry skin and a bottle of Drambuie. Henri called to see that I was safely home. How thoughtful everyone was. The next day, I thought, *I must get some mail written and contact some more people.* Duties and more duties. Maybe I could find time to visit the Borghese gardens and museum. I wished I could share this with Henri, but he had no time. Everyone wanted him and seemed to know him. I guess he was a celebrity in Rome (a celibate celebrity)! I heard the sisters speaking of him and his weekly radio program. I kept thinking of the Priscilla catacomb and the comfortable feeling I had while I was down there. Why did it seem so right and not at all scary? This had been another special day in my life.

May 18

I wrote this entry a day late as the events of a very full and unusual day prevented me from writing. In the morning, I walked to St. Peter's and mailed some cards home, came back for lunch, and walked to the Piazza del Popolo, where so many demonstrations had taken place. Little did I know that I would be back at that very piazza later in the evening.

Some friends at home had me promise to look up their friends in Rome. I had finally contacted them, and they invited me to their penthouse after dinner. Their home was above a theater and overlooked the Piazza del Popolo. The elevator to the penthouse was frightening. The lattice-grated elevator car had no solid walls and zoomed through the ceiling of the theater, up to their glass-walled home looking out on all of Rome. As we visited, we discovered a common interest in catacombs. They showed me photos of some recently discovered catacombs that were under a nearby street. An early artist had copied some paintings found there from ones in the Priscilla catacombs. Before saying good night, I delivered a letter from their American friends.

A taxi took me home after midnight. The convent door was bolted! My key was of no use. No one lived on the lower levels, and I knew the telephone was in an outer hallway, where it might not be heard. I had never felt so alone. I, a woman, alone in Rome, who couldn't speak Italian and who didn't bring her passport (foolishly left in the room), with youthful gangs hanging around—I was a bit scared.

With my only gettone coin for the telephone, I tried to call Henri from a night café, hoping he could raise someone at the convent. But the monastery's porter would not put my call through. He said it was too late. I knew it was too late; that's why I was worried. I needed help! Rome was no place to be alone, especially as a woman, and at this time of crisis, with the Red Brigades causing so much trouble.

The porter wanted to know if this call was from America. I said, "Yes, this is an American calling."

That seemed to satisfy him, and Henri answered. God, his Dutch accent never sounded better! He arranged for a taxi to take me to his brotherhood's residence where he, another priest, and four seminarians sat around, calling hotels until they found one that would take me in. Henri put on an old raincoat; we hopped into a taxi and were at the Hotel Michelangelo in five minutes.

The hotel clerk tried to charge me twenty-four thousand liras, but Henri said, "No, it is too much." The clerk said "Twelve thousand lira" and asked for my passport, which was still back at the convent. Henri grew angry and spoke to him with such authority that anyone in the world would have obeyed. The clerk demanded the money then. Henri said, "No, tomorrow." The clerk asked if Henri did not trust him.

At this point, I had forgotten my embarrassment and was admiring this assertive priest. I wondered how he would reply to this. Henri asked, "Are you here in the morning when this lady leaves? No? Then she will pay in the morning!" Suddenly I could see myself having to pay twenty-four thousand liras that night and then another twenty-four thousand in the morning if I had been alone. It was still a man's world.

Henri Nouwen in Rome

May 19

In the morning, on the hotel elevator going down for breakfast, a friendly large man introduced himself. David Schoetz, a lawyer from Wisconsin, was visiting to see the Vatican before heading home after a trip to Africa. He had been in Kenya to attend the ordination of the bishop of Kenya. His family had given the bishop a scholarship when he was first studying to become a priest.

Before getting to breakfast, Mr. Schoetz invited me to see his unusual collection of artifacts from Kenya. He was so enthusiastic with his souvenirs. I wondered where he was going to hang the huge spears and when he would wear such colorful clothes once he got back to America. You meet the most interesting people in Rome. We breakfasted together, and he helped me secure a taxi back to the convent. There had been some consternation among the sisters over my absence, though Henri had called them at 6:00 a.m. to tell them what had happened.

That afternoon, Henri and I had lunch. I gave him a small gift, a special liqueur, for the inconvenience I had caused him the night before. We started the meal outside at a small garden restaurant, but he decided it was too noisy, so we moved indoors. He was finally able to hear more details of my ongoing spiritual journey. His thoughts were that if I truly accepted the revelation, I must be strong enough to believe it through whatever obstacles and problems that might arise. I would meet some people who would think I was crazy, he said. Others would be indifferent, some would believe me, and still others would try to use me. He asked if I was prepared to accept the consequences of this revelation. I did not know.

I left Henri at the college library, near the lovely Trevi Fountain. Sister Charles Marie, the college librarian, met me, and she and I headed home. Later, another sister took me to the telephone exchange to call my friends in La Spezia. It took half an hour to connect the call. There was difficulty and some confusion due to the language translation, but we came to understand that someone there had recently died. Would I please take a train tomorrow to visit them? Of course I would. It meant that I would have to rearrange the rest of my itinerary, but I was more than willing. I wondered who had died. Was it part of the political situation? Off to bed with a stomachache.

May 20

I felt miserable this morning and slept much too long. The sisters were wonderful. Sister Wanda looked so sweet as she came into my room with a rose in a bud vase, two bottles of black pills, a bottle of mineral water, a glass, and a hammer. A hammer? The hammer, I discovered, was to crush the charcoal pills. She gave me the ground charcoal in water to drink and some sulfur pills. What an angel of mercy she was! I was so weak the sisters begged me not to go. I managed to dress and walk to the taxi. Sister Charles Marie rode with me to the train and got me settled in a first-class seat. I was off to La Spezia!

My friends, the Pizzuto family, met me at the station and drove me to their home. They had hosted my daughter several years earlier as part of the American Field Service student exchange program. Their children had grown so tall since the last time I had seen photos of them.

We had dinner and talked of the recent death in their family, Italy's current crisis, and hopes for the future. I extended an invitation for their children to come for a visit to America someday.

The Pizzuto family

May 21

I caught the 11:11 a.m. train back to Rome. I was feeling better but worried about my friends and their country's precarious political situation. I arrived in Rome in time for the 4:00 p.m. meeting of a charismatic group I had heard about before I left the United States. A bus from the railroad station took me to the general location. I saw a group of sisters in a variety of habits hurrying along. When I asked for directions, they told me to follow them. Before the meeting began, I met an inspiring young woman named Ginny Cox. She invited me to sit with her in the inner circle of a large group of priests, laymen, students, nuns, and tourists, all singing praises to the Lord. There must have been over two hundred people.

Near the end of the meeting, there was a disruption to the general good feelings when three Africans in native costumes spoke from various sections of the room. They voiced their concerns about prayer becoming decadent because capitalism had infiltrated. They believed our prayers would not be answered. Another said that capitalism had invaded the group and fewer people would come. I was beginning to seethe with emotion.

A sister commented that there was no reason to bring politics into prayer. She said she felt the need to speak even though she had promised herself she would not this week. But she had thought of Paul on the road to Corinth. When I heard that, I knew Priscilla was reaching through time to move me to speak (she and her husband, Aquila, were with Paul in Corinth). My neck grew tight, and my pulse was racing. But I stood up, turned to everyone, and said, "*Capitalism* is a beautiful word. It means free enterprise for all!"

I sat down amid mixed reactions, and the meeting ended with a final song. Afterward, an Italian American Jesuit priest of the Pontifical Gregorian University came to me and said that he admired what I had done. He understood how difficult it had been for me to speak. He went on to say that many of them thought the same way but lacked the courage to say it. I had broken the spell of negativism. "Good for you," he said. I was very grateful for his encouraging words. Two of my favorite sisters were there and escorted me home, saying something about how my knees might be capped. As we rode the bus past a quaint street lined with gaslights, we spotted an antiques festival. The sisters quickly followed me as I jumped from the bus to have a look. I think they were surprised and enjoyed my impulsiveness.

Returning to the convent, I was determined to get back to my work with Priscilla. Just then, Sister Joan, from the Netherlands, came to my room to hear about Priscilla. She told me of a Professor Rijn who was an authority on the Old and New Testament and the Jews. It happened that his office was in the SIDIC (Service International de Documentation Center). I had intended to meet with Sister Edward, who was in the same building the next day, and hoped I could make the connection with him as well. I had also wanted to paint a picture of the Roman Forum that day, but I felt I needed to meet these people. The hour was late. I was tired and hoped my mind would be clearer after a night's sleep.

May 22

I cashed some traveler's checks at the bank, ran into two acquaintances from America, and did some more reading about Priscilla. The rest of the day was to be filled by an appointment with the Italian American Jesuit priest I had met the evening prior and then later a tea with Sister Edward. I had hoped to recruit the Jesuit priest as a supporter of Priscilla's message, but he was not interested. I was not able to accomplish what I had wanted in this meeting.

When I asked for the time, I found I was already twenty minutes late for my next appointment at SIDIC. I hurried to Sister Edward, only to find that teatime had passed. They assumed I was not coming. I apologized profusely, and Sister Edward was most gracious to treat me to a cup of tea in the kitchen. She made me comfortable and was a good listener. She was most forgiving and a very precious person. She also mentioned that I should meet Father Rijn, a theologian on Hebrew and Christian literature. This was the second suggestion within twenty-four hours to meet this man. In many ways, I felt unequal to my task and wondered if Father Rijn might be the one God would send to help me.

I spent the rest of the day at the college for priests, looking through all the books I could, including some on the Dead Sea Scrolls. Back at the convent, Sister Juanita recognized my fatigue and met me with a hug. She showed such compassion! She gave me a message from Henri. He would meet me in a few days, on Thursday, at 10:45 a.m., to go down into the Scavi. How exciting! We would be under St. Peter's, where the excavations were being done.

May 23

I rose early and was at the Vatican by 8:00 a.m., and I entered St. Peter's and wandered throughout. Behind a statue, I found a staircase under the altar and decided to see where it led. At the bottom of the stairs, I came across a curved corridor with various small chapels. Each held one or two priests deep in prayer. Returning upstairs to the main body of the church, I found a large procession of bishops and cardinals. I counted fifty-six rows of men, four abreast. It was very impressive. Many wore gold chasubles and either red or purple caps. A man wearing a red chasuble and miter cap followed them.

The huge basilica was empty of others except for a priest, one man, and another lone woman. I asked if any of them spoke English, and the woman responded. We talked about the processional, and she inquired about me. She seemed genuinely interested in my research about Priscilla. At the time, I had no idea she was a nun. Hearing that I was staying at a convent, she said that I must have been overdosed with sisters and priests. Eventually, she shyly confessed that she too was a sister! Another sister? It seemed I was in the habit of meeting women who were not in theirs. After we had talked an hour or so, she told me she was Sister Catherine Lafferty of Notre Dame, head of communications for a group concerned with women in religion. She gave me her address, and we planned to meet again.

On my way back to the convent, I had a bit of a fright. A young man followed me for quite a distance. I stopped to look in a store window. In the reflection of the glass, I saw him also stop. I backtracked and took an irregular course, and still he was there. It was not my imagination. It was interesting to feel my doubts about his following me transform to a genuine concern as I tried to evade him. I turned a corner, trying to keep my mind on where I was so as to not become lost.

My concern was that he might try to snatch my purse, so I ducked into a restaurant, walked to the back of a counter, and emptied the contents of my purse into all my pockets. Then I peeked out the doorway, walked quickly down some old streets, and went back down a road to the Trevi Fountain, where some people were gathering. I was near Sister Charles's library, so I ran up the stairs and inside. Safe at last! There at the entrance was Giorgio, who had driven me to the convent when I had first arrived in Rome. He was a welcome familiar face.

I visited Sister Charles and did some more research on Hebrews. I discovered that the Dead Sea Scrolls were found near Qumran. I also read that not all the archaeological findings and manuscripts from Qumran are accessible to scholars or to the public.

Sister Charles gave me a book from Henri on the art of Michelangelo and a note. Before I knew it, Henri was standing next to me. We discussed the path I would need to take for my quest to continue. My journey seemed to be populated by the right people turning up at just the right time. If I were to write a book, all these coincidences would seem unrealistic. There seemed to be too many coincidences. It could only be the hand of God. But it was comforting to know I had other witnesses.

Before I returned home, I needed to see two more people, Sister Catherine of Notre Dame (whom I had met at St. Peter's) and Father Rijn. I hoped that God would continue to provide.

May 24

This morning I called Sister Catherine, and she invited me to visit her home the next day. She asked me to bring my manuscript. That sounded encouraging. Sister Edward called from SIDIC to say Father Rijn's mother had died and he had to go back home to Holland. Though I was sorry for his loss, it made for one less person to hear my story and possibly help me with my quest.

Later in the day, I had time to get caught up on all my personal chores—hairdresser, cleaners, shoe repair (Italian streets are rough on shoes), washing, letters, and a visit to the record store to deliver a letter from another friend in America. (This record store was bombed after I returned home.) I received a gift of a record album for my effort. While waiting for the bus at the busy Piazza Venezia, I had a surprise. Henri appeared out of the crowd and turned his face toward mine. "What are you doing here so early in the day?" he asked. It is such a small world. How in so many places and with so many people and at this particular minute in time could he appear? I was so surprised I blubbered something inane in reply.

My only skirt was at the cleaners, so I shopped to buy another for the following day's visit to Sister Catherine. Before lunch, I spent some time basking in the sun on the convent's terrace. It was lovely. Lunch was sauerkraut soup and surprisingly good. No wonder the food did not have an Italian flavor—this convent's order of nuns was Polish, and only two of them spoke English, so table talk was limited for me. The floor I lived on was for visiting nuns who came for a renewal program or to learn Hebrew or Italian at one of the universities. Fortunately for me, many of these other visiting nuns spoke English fluently.

That afternoon, I sketched a picture for Sister Juanita for her to include in her final papers for a course she was taking from Henri. Sister

Juanita was a warm woman whose eyes spoke of love. She and I, along with a young priest, had gone to a festival one evening in the rain. As I witnessed the sister and the priest interacting, they seemed to enjoy each other's company. I felt they were made for each other, but they could not see it. Or perhaps they would not permit themselves such thoughts.

In return for my sketch, Sister Juanita gave me a lovely St. Joseph cross and allowed me to read her paper on *The Velveteen Rabbit* by M. Williams. It was a delightful children's story from Australia about a toy rabbit wanting to be human and willing to take on the burden of human death to have the joy of being alive.

May 25

I met Henri at 10:30 a.m. as he was arranging my visit to the Scavi, the necropolis under the Vatican basilica, where Saint Peter and so many others are buried. I felt sad and depressed. I was bemoaning my helpless ways and questioning my worthiness for this mission. Henri scolded me for my feelings. How could I tell him I was overwhelmed and feeling unworthy of it all after he and everyone had done so much for me? Deeply frustrated, Henri nearly shouted that God and many people had continually helped me, could I not see it? What more did I want? I needed this emotion. It was a positive expression to shake me up and encourage me to go on.

Step-by-step I climbed down three stories below St. Peter's from the world of today into the world of yesterday. Deep in the bowels of St. Peter's, I felt more sanctified than I did on the upper floors with all the magnificent art and treasures. Down there was the simplicity and faith of centuries. I had stepped into the age of Priscilla, Peter, and Paul. I picked up a small chunk of plaster from within a few feet of where St. Peter's bones had first lain. It smelled two thousand years old! The guide, one of Henri's students, said in just the two years he had been a guide, he had noticed the color of the frescos fading. Time and tourists were taking their toll on the ancient art.

Back aboveground, I once again mentally shifted centuries to the present and went to the Trans World Airlines office to change my ticket to depart from Rome instead of Milan. Later, Sister Catherine picked me up for a beautiful day and evening in the countryside.

Sister Catherine's home was a lovely modern convent. From the roof, we looked out over the green countryside, where shepherds were watching their flocks of grazing sheep. There was a deep, rich smell of grasses. The panoramic sight and smells were incredible. They stimulated all my senses. This was a scene that had been painted many times over the centuries. And here it was still, timeless, like a picture postcard.

She was a great listener and seemed genuinely interested in the possibility of Priscilla's authorship. Sister Catherine suggested I contact Sister Elisabeth Carroll at the Center of Concern in Washington, DC, and offered to write a letter of introduction. She thought that within ten years, women would become priests. These ideas were new and wonderful to me. I enjoyed our visit, discussions, and dinner. The ride home was also interesting. Along the highway leading into Rome, every half mile or so, I saw little beds of red coals burning in the dark. When I asked about this, Sister Catherine laughed and told me to look more closely into the darkness. Looking more closely, I could see statuesque girls wearing short shorts standing in the shadows near the fires. In the miles ahead, these beauties of the shadows lined the road until we reached the center of the city. They were the whores of Rome!

It was after 10:00 p.m. when I returned, but I had called ahead this time for someone to unlock the convent door. There was a message to call Henri. He wanted to know how the day he had planned for me had gone and asked what I thought of the Scavi. I told him how the visit held such deep meaning and significance for me. He was in good spirits. We joked and laughed over my day's excursions. I truly enjoyed talking with him. It was very different from the morning when he had scolded me—*too severely*, I thought—for my lack of faith.

May 26

I had a morning appointment with Prof. Rev. Albert Vanhoye at the Pontifical Biblical Institute. He was a contributing writer to the *Jerome Bible Commentary*. When we met, I did not know that he had done his thesis on The Letter to the Hebrews. As I explained the research I was doing on Priscilla and my belief of her authorship of The Letter to the Hebrews, his demeanor became very formal and conservative. At that point, I realized how inadequate and ineffective I was in expressing myself to him. Later, knowing his background, I could understand his attitude. Henri had tried to prepare me to expect such reactions, but I was still naive. Again, I questioned why I, an artist, was chosen to do this unfamiliar theological and scholarly work.

I met Henri at the Gregorian library. They had set aside a beautiful room for him where he could study, plan, and write. The room was large, rising a story and a half, and had ladders to reach books on the upper shelves. A dark mahogany railing framed the upper levels. The table where he worked was also of dark mahogany and spanned about fifteen feet. It was a quiet and magnificent sanctuary. I relayed my experiences and had him close his eyes to smell the musty little rock I picked up in the Scavi. He listened and then encouraged me. A priest can be an enabler and a bridge. Henri was all that and more!

Before I left, Henri signed his books *The Wounded Healer* and *Reaching Out* for me to present to the convent for its library.

I had planned to go to the Borghese gardens, but it was raining. It seemed I was fated to not see them. At lunch in a small café, I met a lady from New Zealand who was also interested in Priscilla and the Scavi. She asked if she might lay her rosary beads upon the rock I had from Peter's tomb. "Of course," I said and watched her take a little of the dirt still on the rock and pinch it onto her beads. It was interesting to see such reverence for just a little dirt. This was insight for me. In the afternoon, I took a bus to the outskirts of town and back to the Spanish Steps to shop for family gifts.

Nearing the end of my visit to Italy, I had finally begun to recognize the ebb and flow of life in Rome, as well as disruptions to the normal routines. There was much unrest, and I could often hear police sirens. There could be many people on the streets, and suddenly I would become aware that there was no one. One day, while waiting for a bus that never came, I wondered where all the usual people were and why I was alone. Typically, the mass transit service was excellent. I eventually spotted buses traveling on adjacent streets outside their usual route through the center of the plaza. I didn't know why the route changed that day but suspected it might have been related to recent terrorist bombings.

May 27

I had mixed emotions about having to leave the next day. Sister Charles and I returned to the Spanish Steps to continue my shopping. I wanted her to choose something to remember me by. She had been my angel. She chose only a card game and some candy. I hurried back to catch a bus for lunch with Henri. A smiling big priest standing next to me on the bus to St. Peter's introduced himself as Friar Cawley from Hong Kong. Later, I met him again when Henri and I rounded a corner. I introduced the two priests, and Father Cawley said he had heard of Henri in Hong Kong! Their attitudes seemed to shift immediately, as though they each had assumed a different personality. I did not care for this at all and wondered what had happened. Did all people play such games with one another?

Henri chose a little restaurant, where we had a bottle of red wine, pasta, spinach, and veal. He handed me more mail to post in the United States and another of his manuscripts to give to Jane. We had a very stimulating conversation. I felt I could say anything to him. We talked about celibacy, marriage, and women's ordinations. It was enlightening for me—I think for him also and for everyone else in the place! He did not seem to realize how loud he could become in his enthusiasm. Every moment and word was special, even when he chased a taxi in the rain, disappeared around the corner, and eventually reappeared in the back of the taxi to say good-bye.

I had my cab drive me once more to the Borghese gardens. I wanted so much to see it, but again it was closed. I felt emptiness and dryness in all the rain, a paradox for sure. I delivered another letter for friends and ended my day by buying roses for Sister Edward. I dropped them in a puddle, no real damage done, and gave them to her anyway in gratitude for her help with Priscilla.

My friends at the convent and I shared our last dinner together. We stayed up late. First, Sister Juanita visited my room, and we cried. Then Sister Charles came to give me encouragement for the trip home. I felt very comfortable in their world, though Rome was very tense with contingents of police throughout the city. Seventeen squad cars sped by. Four parked at our bus stop. Sister Charles told me she was going to find her own apartment. It was strange how the tension affected each one of us. Yet I was reluctant to leave the place in which I had felt so very close to Priscilla. I didn't know if I would lose that feeling after I left the sights and sounds of Rome.

As I thought back over my time in this wonderful city, I realized that each day had been very special. I had been privileged to share briefly in the lives of so many dedicated people. All had touched my life in their own way, helped me on my journey, and left an imprint that I would cherish always.

Interwoven with these feelings was the realization that I had proved nothing about Priscilla. Or had I? Was this to be the end of my journey in pursuit of establishing Priscilla's authorship of The Letter to the Hebrews? Little did I know that one photo I had taken would reveal a long-lost secret, would continue my spiritual journey, and would take me back to Rome.

CHAPTER SIX

Home—Just the Beginning

Back home, in June of 1978, I found it difficult to readjust my approach to life. I begged God to not let me down too fast. The lifestyle at the Roman convent had been quite different from that of my hometown, Hamden, Connecticut. My intense and continuous search for spiritual connections to Priscilla, which seemed so important and promising in Italy, didn't seem to have the same significance at home. Rather, it felt like an exercise in futility. The impact of the beautiful revelation was over, or so it seemed.

I had been prepared for the normal letdown one usually experiences after a mountaintop adventure, but I was still disappointed to feel so profoundly directionless and remote from Priscilla. Yet I wondered, Why had I been led so many thousands of miles away? Why had I been the recipient of so much encouragement and guidance? All this for what purpose? It seemed unlikely that it was all for nothing. God certainly had intervened in my life. It was as if I had been given the clues to a mystery then challenged to solve it. Each day in Rome, I felt information had been gleaned from every possible source. I would say, "There is nothing more to be learned. It is finished." But then something new would happen. More knowledge, more enthusiasm, a new situation would present itself and lead me in a new direction. I wondered what more I could find now that I was home, in the United States.

I was home only a few days when a letter arrived from Rome to gladden my heart.

Sister Joan D—
Via di Monte Cucco
Roma, Italy

My Dear Carolyn,

How disappointed I was when I came back Sunday evening and was told you went home! The first thing I did was to go upstairs to your room, but it was empty!

Now Carolyn, this morning I went into a book shop and saw a small book, The Daily Study Bible: The Letter to the Hebrews *by William Barclay (the Saint Andrews Press Edinbury [sic]). It has a brown cover. See that you get it! I did buy it and started to read it just one hour ago. In the introduction it said; the author of Hebrews:*

1. *Tertullian thought that Barnabas wrote it.*
2. *Luther was sure that Apollos was the author.*
3. *The most romantic of all conjecture is that of Harnack, the Great German Scholar. He thought that maybe Aquila and Priscilla wrote it between them. Harnack thought that is why The Letter begins with no greetings and why the writer's name has vanished because the main author of Hebrews was a woman and women were not allowed to teach.*

When I read this I thought that I have to write Carolyn. Thus, your next step is to try to come in contact with Harnack. A German scholar can speak and write English! Go on. Prove!! I am a Dutch woman and believe you fully. I'll pray for you and your message! May God bless you.

Much love from Sr. Joan.

While this letter was validating and encouraging, I still did not expect that I would discover more as a result of my trip to Italy. But the letter's sincerity gave me the energy to continue my research.

The photo slides that I had taken in Rome were my solace. They proved that I had been there, even to the very burial niche in which

Priscilla was interred and the catacomb that had served as an early church. They proved I had walked in many of the same places as Priscilla, Aquila, and Paul. We had seen the same frescos in the catacombs. My travels were a pilgrimage that I needed to make. Just as a student of military history needs to visit battle sites to make their lessons real, I needed to see the Priscilla catacomb. My slides were a good reminder. I studied each picture and recalled all my experiences.

Of all the many slides, one in particular drew my attention. It was not taken in the Priscilla catacombs but in an ancient part of the two-thousand-year-old Church of St. Prassede. The photo was of a beautiful gold mosaic in the oratory of the St. Zeno Chapel. Checking my Roman diary, I found the entry describing my visit to that particular church with my guide, Dan Sanders.

The mosaic was a portrait of four women, each of them with a halo. One of the women, however, had a square halo, indicating that the individual had been *alive* when sainted, as I had learned in my classes of religion in art. The four figures are said to be depictions of the Virgin Mary, sister saints Prassede and Pudentiana on each side of her, and Theodora, the mother of Pope Paschal. Theodora was sainted while still living, thus the square halo.[48] Prassede and Pudentiana, from the Pudens family, were probably the younger cousins or nieces of the Priscilla married to Aquila. They were also the granddaughters of the Priscilla married to Roman senator Quintus Cornelius Pudens, who was also the namesake of, and first to be buried in, the Priscilla catacombs. These granddaughters of Priscilla Pudens were declared saints shortly after their deaths. The early church considered all martyrs to be saints, as well as other members who suffered for their faith. The lengthy modern process of canonization for saints was not developed until a thousand years later.

Later, during the time of Pope Gregory, several women named Priscilla, including Priscilla Pudens and the Priscilla married to Aquila, were combined and regarded as one Saint Priscilla.

How I wished that one of those figures could have been my Priscilla. How appropriate it would have been for her to be there with her sainted relatives. It would have been a fitting tribute.

Four women saints at the St. Zeno chapel, church of St. Prassede

I wanted to share this with my husband, but he was on the telephone. As I waited impatiently for his conversation to end, I picked up a book called *The Early Christians in Rome* by Henry Donald Maurice Spence-Jones.[49] It opened to page 264–265, right where he was discussing the saints that were in the mosaic. He tells how the Pudens family created a small meeting place, or oratory, in their house, and how it was later expanded into a church. He quoted from the *Liber Pontificalis* (second recension) under Pope Pius I (AD 142–157, extracted from Acts of SS. Pudentianae et Praxedis.

> *Then Pudentiana went to God. Her sister (Prassedis) and I (Pastor) wrapped her in perfumes, and kept her concealed in the oratory. Then after 28 days we carried her to the Cemetery of Priscilla and laid her near her father Pudens.*[50]

A note is added of the death of Novatus, her brother, who bequeathed his goods to Prassedis, who then erected a church in his baths. The ancient record continues,

> *At the end of two years a great persecution was declared against*
> *Christians, and many of them received the crown of martyrdom.*
> *Prassedis concealed a great number of them in her oratory . . .*
> *The Emperor Antoninus heard of these meetings in the oratory*
> *of Prassedis, and many Christians were taken . . . The blessed*
> *Prassedis collected their bodies by night and buried them in the*
> *Cemetery of Priscilla . . . Then the Virgin of the Saviour, worn*
> *out with sorrow, only asked for death. Her tears and her prayers*
> *reached to heaven, and 54 days after her brethren had suffered,*
> *she passed to God. And I, Pastor, the priest, have buried her*
> *body near that of her father Pudens.*[51]

Surely it was more than coincidence that I opened to these particular pages in a book that had been available to me before. It was, I am convinced, another example of God encouraging me to continue on the path I had embarked upon by going to Rome. These four historic and notable women staring at me from the mosaic, two of whom were from Priscilla's family, were daring me to continue my spiritual journey. I believed in Priscilla before I embarked on my year of searching for documentation. Now, God had led me another step forward in faith and given me the vision to see Priscilla and her family in the context of her own heritage.

I continued on to the slides I had taken in the Priscilla catacombs. I could immediately see that each painting on the ancient walls represented a passage from chapter 11 of her letter to the Hebrews. Each was intended as a statement of faith. Her message to all people exhorted them to have faith in God to demonstrate the great faith shown by their ancestors, who faced death in the mouths of hungry lions or in the violence of fire. She believed that strength could come out of weakness and that we must work to make faith strong. This is why chapter 11, which defined and illustrated faith through the lives of the Old Testament heroes, was so important and had such significance! How clear it all became to me. For here in her catacombs, the paintings were reaching out to amplify her words in her letter to the Hebrews 11:1:

> *Now faith is the assurance of things hoped for, the conviction*
> *of things not seen.*[52]

CHAPTER SEVEN

A Discovery

Gradually, my life fell into its normal pattern, though Priscilla was seldom far from my thoughts. Occasionally, I was asked to show the slides from my trip. Each time I showed them and spoke about my experiences, I found it slightly disturbing. On the one hand, I felt my journey of discovery was over. On the other, I had a feeling that there was still something else to uncover. And once again, a particular image kept haunting me. Whenever I showed the slides, it would command more and more of my attention. I would always promise myself that I would look at it more closely after I got home. But each time, it was too late in the day or I would be too tired to unpack the slide tray, and I would put the matter aside.

Four months after my return from Rome, another facet of Priscilla's amazing legacy was revealed to me. Science was about to enter my religious and spiritual journey. Early one afternoon, I received a call that Henri's mother, Maria, had died. I thought back to Rome and remembered having a chill go through me and a premonition when Henri pointed to the place where Maria had recently fallen in the street. With the news of her death, I knelt beside my bed to say a prayer for her and all the sadness in the world. I must have been more tired than I knew.

When I awoke after a short but seemingly timeless sleep, I was refreshed and filled with memories of Rome. My thoughts immediately went to my tray of slides. Curiosity, renewed energy, and clarity of thought sent me looking for the one slide I wanted to reexamine more closely. I found it and placed it into a small handheld projector. My anticipation was followed by exhilaration. I had found something!

Man pointing to apple/star

The photo was of an ancient fresco on a ceiling inside the Priscilla catacombs. The burnt sienna pigments depicted a man (prophet) standing next to the world's oldest known image of the Madonna and child. He was pointing over the Madonna's head to what appeared to be a large apple. It was part of an adjacent fresco of apple trees, which formed an arch above a shepherd and his sheep. The apple tree scene was perpendicular to the one of the pointing man and the Madonna and child. When I turned the photo so that the Madonna and child were upright, the apples seemed to belong to that scene as well. A shepherd and sheep, a Madonna and child, and a vast array of apples scattered above. A man depicted standing next to the Madonna was pointing to a particularly large and bright apple above the Madonna's head. Together they brought to mind so many elements of the nativity! Could the fruit on the trees be stars disguised as apples?

Double fresco

The practice of astrology and astronomy were forbidden in those days. Anyone finding a message in the stars and wanting to record and convey it for posterity would certainly have had to find a way to hide their message and intent. My excitement mounted as I contemplated the arrangement of the apples.

I had an idea. Abandoning the image for a moment, I drove to the library and borrowed a book called *The Stars* by H. A. Rey. I could hardly wait to get home to check out my hunch. From my limited knowledge of astronomy, I knew there was a constellation called Aquila. Since that had been Priscilla's husband's name, could there be a link?

As I studied the book, it seemed to me that, as I had anticipated, the apples were arranged similarly as the stars in the constellation Aquila. My husband suggested that I do a tracing and compare. This served to verify what my artist's eye had already perceived. I could hardly believe what I was discovering! The painting would have had to be done by someone who was an authority on the stars.

I speculated that a relative of Priscilla who practiced astrology/ astronomy, even though it was against Christian belief and Roman law, felt compelled to record yet conceal stars' positions above the picture of the Madonna and child.

In my tracing, each apple matched a star in the Aquila constellation. Each apple matched, with one exception! In this two-thousand-year-old fresco, there was one star not in the sky today! The large prominent apple that the man next to the Madonna was pointing to had no counterpart in my astronomy book. It had to be the star of Bethlehem! I knew then the exhilaration that all discoverers felt. A moment of illumination and truth! But what would I do with this knowledge? Who would listen?

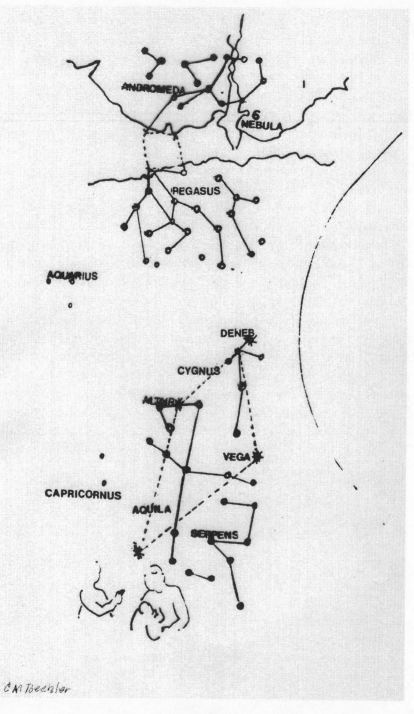

Fresco key

I called on Charles "Kelly" H. Clark, the dean of the Berkeley Divinity School at Yale. Trying to suppress my enthusiasm, I showed him the catacomb picture and had him compare it to the tracing I made over it to reveal the hidden constellation of Aquila. He responded that I should write a paper about my discovery. His suggestion was disappointing and not at all what I wanted to hear. I was an artist, not a scholar or writer. Such a task seemed insurmountable.

To talk myself out of a funk, I thought, *Surely, none of us should become discouraged with our work.* Priscilla had shown me that there is always value in making an attempt. Once something has been attempted, there is always hope for its fulfillment, even if it comes after your death. I thought, *As long as there is life, there is hope, but there is still hope after life as well.*

If I had felt completely out of my depth researching religion and history, I was absolutely at a loss when it came to astronomy. Yet God had been with me all along my journey. He had shown me the way and provided earthly angels to help. Little did I know that just as distinguished and learned religious leaders had unexpectedly appeared when I needed them, so too would respected scholars in the fields of astronomy and other sciences. But I had to struggle on my own for several months before this help was to come. In the interim, I was called to seek out and connect with some great women of faith.

CHAPTER EIGHT

Equal Rites for Women

The task of documenting my discoveries and spiritual journey seemed, to me, to be a gargantuan and onerous one. Yet sooner than I would have thought, I had the beginnings of a document to share with others. Many of the people I had met along the way would continue to help me with the manuscript and by making important new connections.

As I was lugging my easel and paints into the RSV room at the Yale Divinity School, I thought about the chain of events that had taken me here. But for an unexpected ride in a mail truck during a snowstorm last winter, I probably would not be teaching the class on Spirituality of Religion in Art. And if it hadn't been for a revelation, a trip to Puerto Rico and then to Rome, and meeting so many wonderful and learned people, I wouldn't have the encouragement to start on my manuscript.

I passed the plaque in the hall dedicated to the people who worked on the Revised Standard Version of the Bible in the very room in which I was teaching. How unfair it seemed that they were recognized for their contributions while Priscilla still remained in obscurity. I dedicated part of my class that day to telling my students about Priscilla and my discovery in the catacombs.

The most recent development in my life was an invitation to the Women's Ordination Conference in Baltimore from Sister Elizabeth Carroll. The woman who had helped me at St. Peter's in Rome, Sister Catherine Lafferty, had suggested I look up Sister Elizabeth Carroll when I returned to the States. After exchanging letters and some phone calls with Sister Elisabeth Carroll, she invited me to the conference. I soon learned that it was for women interested in becoming priests! Doubt began to set in. What would I do there? I wasn't even Catholic.

The morning I was to leave for the conference, I was depressed. It was 9:00 a.m., and I was still in bed. Negative thoughts were dominating me. What did it matter if I met these women? How could it help Priscilla or them? On top of everything, I had also made an appointment to meet Professor Dorothy Taylor Durand at Douglass Residential College (Rutgers University) in New Jersey along the way. A friend suggested I meet her for possible help with my manuscript. I would have to be on the road by nine thirty if I were to keep both engagements. I would cancel the trip. I needed a sign from somewhere to move me or I was going to stay in bed.

My depression turned to utter boredom in the stillness of the room. So very bored. I could not tolerate it. Suddenly, I jumped from bed, threw on some clothes, drank some orange juice, grabbed my manuscript, and sped toward the turnpike to keep my appointments. I would at least keep the appointment in New Jersey, if not Baltimore. The traffic flowed smoothly. As the landscape went zooming by, I reflected on life with Priscilla. As I was driving over the George Washington Bridge with no heavy traffic, my outlook on life took a sudden upturn.

The meeting at Douglass Residential College with Professor Durand went well. She seemed genuinely interested, and I was able to leave her a copy of my manuscript. After the meeting, I had a decision to make. If I headed home, I would be crossing the George Washington Bridge at rush hour and in the dark. Or I could head south to Baltimore. I called my husband, Dan, to see how he felt about it. He knew and understood what I had to do, so south it was.

I stopped along the way and called ahead to the conference's program director. The hotels were filled with over two thousand sisters and laypeople, and I needed someone to find me a place to sleep. The program director said she could help, and I, without a suitcase, drove on to Baltimore.

When I arrived, the hotel clerk told me how to find the program director. I stepped out of an elevator to find myself in a hallway with a startling banner that announced Priests for Equality. I was surprised. I had always thought that all priests supported equality and did not know that there were priests who did not! I clutched a noisy paper bag, which held a pair of new department store pajamas and a toothbrush bought from a vending machine, and entered a lecture hall filled with people listening to a priest.

How would I recognize the program director, or she me? I slipped into a seat and wrote on the back of one of my personal cards, "Please pass this note along unless you are the program director." It was fun watching the note being read and passed along until it stopped three rows ahead of me on the far side of the hall. When a woman looked up and searched the room with her eyes, I knew she was the one. She had made arrangements for me to share a room with a nun in the hotel.

Later that night, my roommate, Sister Sue, spoke of her work at the copper mines. She told me how she had given last rites to a young man she knew who had his legs blown off in an explosion deep in the mines. With the severed legs still propped in a corner, she held and comforted him until he died. I once thought sisters were sweet flowers in a garden. But this popular impression misrepresents their brave and ambitious work for God. Sister Sue was only one example of the brave women who had dedicated their lives to Christian service for two thousand years. That weekend I witnessed thousands of women who were enthusiastic, loving, and strong in their love of God. It opened my eyes even more to the truth that churches have not fully accepted this great gift from God—women!

The next day when I moved into the hotel in Baltimore, I saw a tall priest trying to count his change while examining the domination of each coin. I went to his aid to help him with the currency, and he introduced himself. Johannes "Hans" Wijngaards was a Dutch priest who had recently served in India for thirteen years and was now the vicar general of the Mill Hill Missionaries in London.

After helping him with his currency, we had breakfast together. It was a beautiful sunny day, and we walked down the harbor to take part in the opening of the conference. Everyone sang songs of famous religious women, and one of the songs mentioned Priscilla. Hundreds of us marched up the main street, each carrying a link of a chain that stretched a mile long. Along the way, Hans noticed the USS *Constellation*, a historic sailing vessel. He had just heard my story of Aquila's constellation in the catacombs and was pleasantly surprised at the coincidence.

The enthusiasm and comradeship of the many women at the conference was inspirational. There were workshops, lectures, and the Holy Eucharist. Everything was extremely well organized. Their theme was Equal Rites for Women.

Hans invited me to dinner, and afterward we spent the evening reviewing my manuscript. We used his bed as our table, spreading out the pages, sifting through references, and consulting my journal. He suggested that I change the narrative structure. He thought that my story and Priscilla's should be interwoven to reflect our spiritual bonds and responses to each other.

At one point, he noticed holes in my stockings. I had no change of clothing, but I knew it was right to not worry about what I was wearing. It was a freedom from concern about my appearance that I had never known before. In his gentle way, Hans removed his shoes and pointed to the holes in his socks. Before I left, I mentioned to Hans that I was leaving for home in the morning. I had hoped to see Sister Elizabeth Carroll and Dr. Elisabeth Schüssler Fiorenza, but their schedules had been very tight, and I did not want to impose upon them. Hans and I then said our good-byes.

The next morning, I was surprised to be told that I had appointments with both women. Unfortunately, both appointments were for the same late hour of the day. I accepted these unexpected gifts, praying that the Lord would solve the timing issue, and went to arrange for another night's lodging. Meeting Hans was such an unexpected blessing. Not only had he encouraged me and helped with ideas for the manuscript, I suspected he also had a hand in my getting the two appointments. With his strong support for women's ordination, the idea of Priscilla as a leader of the early church and author of The Letter to the Hebrews naturally appealed to him. We corresponded periodically after he returned to England. His belief in and passion for the cause was so great that I believe when, in 1998, Pope John Paul II banned discussion of women's ordination, Hans resigned from the priestly ministry.

Now I was faced with the dilemma of having to be in two places at the same time and at the opposite ends of huge Baltimore Civic Center. I decided to see Dr. Elizabeth Carroll first. After first hearing about her from Sister Catherine Lafferty in Rome and many months of writing and calling, we finally greeted each other. As we clasped hands, I explained to her that I had an appointment at the same moment with

Dr. Elisabeth Schüssler Fiorenza. She replied that this was not a problem as we could go and meet with her also.

As we turned to go, there, walking toward us, smiling, in this large assembly of women was Sister Catherine Lafferty! She had been the one to suggest that Elizabeth Carroll and I meet, and here she was, all the way from Rome, witnessing it happen. For her to be at the exact spot at the exact moment was a miracle. After meeting up with Dr. Elisabeth Schüssler Fiorenza, the four of us attended Mass and took communion together and shared the very special, precious moment God had given us. I shared my research about Priscilla with them and went away greatly encouraged.

While at the conference, I had more opportunities to share my information about Priscilla and what I thought was a sky chart in her catacomb. What impression it made, I did not know, but I was privileged to meet and speak with so many influential modern theologians. And so many coincidences!

Sunday morning, I was about to leave for home when the registration desk attendant asked if I would do an evaluation of the conference. She noticed the address on my name tag and asked if I was leaving soon. If so, could I give someone a ride? I agreed, and she introduced me to Robert Werner from Colorado, who needed a ride to New Haven. A friend was waiting for him there. "You see," he said, "I have an appointment this evening with Henri Nouwen, and I would like to make his Mass at nine p.m."

I was stunned. Since I had begun letting God lead me, my life had become so exciting and wonderful. I never would have believed it could be this way. The adventures, the wonderful people, the perfect timing, the energy, and the happy glow I felt were the gifts God gave to me. He was saying, "Is there any person in your world that can give you the excitement and thrills that I can give you when you believe in me?" I was filled with the Lord's blessing.

On the drive to New Haven, Robert told me about how he had helped Henri with *The Genesee Diary* and that Henri had acknowledged him in the book. I told him about the painting I had given to Henri and that it was my interpretation of Thoreau's "If a man does not keep pace with his companions, it may be that he keeps pace with a different drummer." Henri had used this quote in *The Genesee Diary*. I let Robert drive so that I could sit back, relax, and fill this captive listener in on the message of Priscilla. Six hours later, we stepped out of the car back in New Haven. We arrived in time to attend Holy Eucharist, with Henri officiating, at Yale's stone tower chapel. Henri gave us a special blessing. He seemed only mildly surprised at Robert's and my chance meeting in Baltimore.

That evening, we learned that Henri would soon be leaving our world and returning to the monastery at Genesee, New York. He had so much to give to his students; I hoped it would be just a temporary retreat.

CHAPTER NINE

Continued Discovery

It had almost been a year since the beginning of my revelation. I had been taken down into the depths of the earth, up into the heavens, and to another dimension of living. Science, religion, art, and history were being drawn together on my personal spiritual journey.

Two months had passed since I first noticed the constellation of Aquila hidden as an apple tree in Priscilla's catacomb. I had worked on my manuscript but was unhappy with its progress. Taking a break from my writing, I opened my weekly *Time* magazine (the December 25, 1978, Christmas issue). I noticed an article titled "Einstein's Wave" in the science section. Reading it, I shook with excitement. Astronomer Joseph H. Taylor and his colleagues had discovered gravitational waves coming from the constellation of Aquila. They were detected as rhythmic radio signals. The source was "a pulsar, or rapidly rotating neutron star—the incredibly compressed cadaver of a giant star." Taylor found it in 1974 using the radio telescope at Arecibo, Puerto Rico. Scientists had been studying it for four years.

This meant that at the same time I was down in the catacomb studying and taking pictures of the apple tree / constellation fresco, these astronomers were examining the same portion of the sky. Using a new, sensitive computerized clock device, they had detected gravitational waves in the constellation of Aquila from a star that was no longer visible to the naked eye.

How interesting that this article should appear at Christmastime and just as I was beginning to think my journey with Priscilla might be coming to an end. This exciting new information moved me to look again at the slide with the double painting. I had thought that my discovery of the constellation hidden in the apples was the completion of the revelation. As I examined the slide, I realized I was not yet finished! How very humble I felt. Again, I had underestimated my Lord.

Beyond the Madonna and shepherd, there was a second apple tree. I compared the apples in this second tree to one of the star charts from a library book to see if they also corresponded to constellations. I discovered that the fruit matched three constellations as they would appear in spring: Cygnus, Pegasus, and a portion of Andromeda! Previously I had only a small portion of the sky. Now with four constellations, this gave me a much broader view. Ancient people used the night sky as their calendar. If the depictions in the fresco were accurate, then not only would it show the season, it could show the month or even day. There was still the mystery of the one large apple in the constellation of Aquila that the man in the fresco was pointing to that did not match!

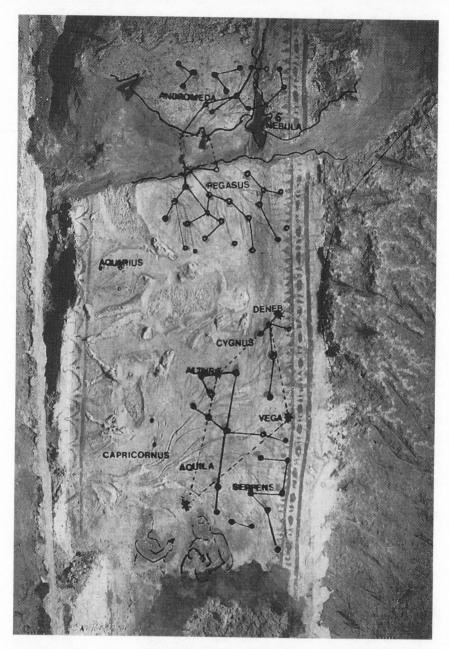

Overlay fresco key

The old biblical story of the shepherds watching their sheep by night entered into my thoughts. Shepherds do watch their sheep at night, especially when they are lambing. Sheep are usually bred in October, and five months later, they give birth in March.

Perhaps the ancient astronomer conceived a way to record the date of an important event by painting the constellations. But the practice of astronomy and astrology was against the Roman law and the Christian faith. Studying the stars, especially to determine one's destiny, was considered a pagan practice. If he created a fresco of the night sky, he could have been banished or imprisoned, and his work and message destroyed. By disguising the constellations as apple trees, he would avoid political and religious trouble and preserve his message for the ages. So effective was this disguise that the message remained secret for two thousand years! If this were all true, then what was the date he was trying to tell us, and what was its significance?

I consulted many resources in the hopes of finding out more about the meaning of the sky chart in the catacomb but found nothing. Not knowing how to proceed, I called my friend Bea MacMullen. Once again, Bea, who had first introduced me to Henri Nouwen, became my angel. She shared my excitement and later called me with a surprise. She had arranged a luncheon date to introduce me to her friend Dr. Dorrit Hoffleit, an astronomer at Yale University.

Over lunch I explained my findings to Dr. Hoffleit. Her apparent lack of reaction to my discovery was disappointing. I wondered where to turn to next. It takes an exceptional person to be open to new ideas. The average person is apt to think that people who have revelations and discover new things are a bit crazy. But later that night, I received an unexpected call from Dr. Hoffleit to say she had some books and information I could use. I was thrilled she had called!

I visited as soon as her schedule allowed. She most graciously showed me the basics of how to read sky charts. We discussed coordinates, right and left ascensions and declinations. One of her books that she thought might be helpful was the *Soviet Catalog of Variable Stars* published by the Astronomical Council of the Academy of Science in the USSR. It contained ancient Chinese sky charts. She loaned me this book and D. A. Bennett's star explorer chart and showed me how to use them. Taking them home, I wondered if I could ever understand enough to make them useful, but she had been a very good teacher.

Studying these materials and the ancient fresco, I was able to estimate the celestial coordinates of the extra apple/star in the catacomb painting. The man standing next to the Madonna was pointing to something above that had a right ascension of twenty hours and a declination of negative twenty. The ancient Chinese sky charts recorded a phenomenon in that general position as comet or nova around March 24–25 in the year 5 BC.

Thinking about the *Time* magazine article and the pulsar near the constellation of Aquila, I decided to call the University of Massachusetts and speak with astronomer Joseph H. Taylor. I wanted to clarify his findings about the remnants of the nova and its exact coordinates. He gave me the pulsar coordinates as right ascension of nineteen hours, thirteen minutes, twelve seconds and declination of twelve hours, one minute, eight seconds. I was disappointed. His coordinates were several degrees off mine. I was hoping for a perfect match.

When I called Dr. Hoffleit, it was a pleasure to hear her laugh with acknowledgment at what I found. She must have known something of what was in the book before she asked me to visit. I explained that I was excited that the positions were in the same proximity but was concerned about the differences. She reassured me that given the semicylindrical shape of the catacomb ceiling, the dim lighting when it was originally painted, and the limitation of the ancient measurements, I shouldn't be concerned about the differences. She thought that the objects were placed within an acceptable degree of accuracy.[53]

The Chinese record showed a comet appearing in the position of the catacomb apple on March 24–25 in 5 BC. In the early days, the Chinese called all unusual sky phenomena as comets. Today, it would be identified as a supernova because unlike comets that travel across the sky, it stayed in one position. The ancient charts showed the supernova as very large, near the eastern horizon, and lasting for seventy-six days—long enough for wise men to follow on foot or by camel. This phenomenon happened in March, the spring season for shepherds in the fields caring and watching the lambing of their sheep both day and night. It must have presented a spectacular view as it was in alignment with the first magnitude stars—Vega, Deneb, and Altair, forming a perfect arrow of the brightest stars.

Clearly, the significance of this sky chart being placed over the oldest known painting of a Madonna and child was to record a historical event. I believe Priscilla, Aquila, or someone of their family who was also a second-generation disciple wanted to record this date to document the birth of Christ as March 24 or 25, 5 BC. How better than to weave it all into a painting in their sacred burial place. Documentation of the true beginning of Anno Domini!

Priscilla, Aquila, or one of their descendants must have wanted a personal and permanent record of this event that had changed their lives and those of thousands of other Christians. The whole story of the development of our Christian heritage and faith was recorded in her letter to the Hebrews. The birth of it was recorded in her catacomb. What safer or more rightful place than in the catacomb that served as one of the first churches of Rome? Here, the sky chart remained visible to worshippers, tourists, and archeologists but remained unseen for nearly two thousand years!

Revelation and science had given me the key to unlock a historical and religious mystery.

Soon after this discovery, I was discussing my findings with the great naturalist Roland Clement, who had studied painting with me. He immediately called his colleague S. Dillon Ripley at the Smithsonian. Mr. Ripley arranged for us to meet *Smithsonian* magazine editor John P. Wiley Jr. He was interested in my story, but like any good editor, he needed to verify my information and sources for accuracy before considering publication. This was wonderful news! If this were published, it would give greater creditability and acceptance for this miraculous revelation and the hidden message buried for two thousand years.

As part of their fact-checking, *Smithsonian* magazine contacted Dorrit Hoffleit at Yale about my discovery. She was my champion! In her reply to John P. Wiley, she assuaged his concerns.

October 31, 1979

Dear Mr. Wiley:

> *Mrs. Carolyn M. Beehler has shown me her identifications of the stars represented on the ceiling of the Priscilla catacomb. Her task was far from easy, but I feel she has done as well as anyone could. I hope you too will feel satisfied.*

Distortions of the star fields are inevitable for a great variety of reasons:

1. *The artist was working in a very dark place, where he must have plotted the star position either from memory or from sketches made outdoors. Both memory and representation could be faulty.*

2. *He must have used lamplight, and it is likely the lamp would not have illuminated all of the ceiling at the same time. This could introduce distortions of one constellation relative to another, particularly as it is unlikely that the whole painting was accomplished in a single sitting.*

3. *If an artist is, for symbolic reasons, particularly concerned with one particular constellation he would naturally emphasize it over others. Thus Aquila could have been made too prominent relative to surrounding constellations (making the normally conspicuous Cygnus too small relative to Aquila).*

4. *The sky is usually thought of as the surface of a sphere. Representing this on a cylindrical surface would introduce some distortion. Actually, I understand, only the top of the ceiling is cylindrical, the total shape of the surface being more nearly that of an inverted U.*

5. *The configurations of the flat sides, where the artist viewed what he was doing horizontally, would have been much easier to paint than those overhead. So besides geometrical perspective effects, some psychological effects might also be introduced, for example resulting from a kink in the neck from looking overhead, or lying supine while painting what was in the zenith.(Effects analogous to the moon illusion on size.)*

6. *A photograph used as the basis for identification could well introduce further distortions, as various parts of the painting would not be at the same focal distance from the camera, and not all parts of the picture would be perpendicular to the line of sight.*

7. *The fact the original painting was partially obliterated by an overpainting at a later date, converting the stars to "apples," undoubtedly destroyed the original representations of the relative brightness of the stars. Hence only the relative distances and directions between the "apples" can be taken into consideration. The original sizes would have been a very helpful criterion.*

Taking all these factors in to account, we should be amazed how well Mrs. Beehler has succeeded in identifying the stars, rather than being distressed that the constellations do not look exactly like our modern star charts. I wonder what artist could have done better in a dark, dank dungeon?!

My apologies for making this so long. Like the prominent author who wrote a novel in two volumes because he did not have time to do it in one; I am momentarily pressed for time to condense this.

I do hope Mrs. Beehler's efforts will now clinch her exciting story to the complete satisfaction of the editor.

Sincerely,
Dorrit Hoffleit

Smithsonian magazine published my discovery in their June 1980 issue. The broad exposure generated interest from around the world. Newspapers, magazines, and academic journals interviewed me and published their own articles. My findings became the subject of academic papers, discussion, and debate. The planetarium at the University of the Pacific created a Christmas show that included my discovery of the star of Bethlehem and the date of Christ's birth. I was even interviewed at length on television!

The articles are the following:

•   Carolyn Beehler, "Catacomb Painting of Trees May Be an Ancient Star Map," *Smithsonian* 11, no. 3 (June 1980): 158–159.

- "The Priscilla Catacomb Painting: A Hidden Star Map Revealed," *Archaeoastronomy* (the bulletin of the Center for Archaeoastronomy) 3, no. 3 (July-August-September 1980): 14–16.

- Carolyn Beehler, "Follow the Star," *United Church of Christ, A.D. Vol 9*, no. 11 (December 1980): 24–25.[1]

This revelation of Priscilla brought me more excitement and wonderment than I ever knew existed. The publication brought many calls for more information, praise, and criticism. My only disappointment was that most of the press, while excited about the sky chart, ignored my revelation and conviction of Priscilla's authorship. I was satisfied nonetheless. Priscilla had led me to all these discoveries for the purpose of opening the boundaries of our faith, and I believed I had been her instrument.

---

[1] A copy of Carolyn's television interview is posted on the Internet on YouTube. Search for "The Priscilla Revelation & the Christmas Star."

CHAPTER TEN

Discovering More History

Priscilla had dominated my life for more than a year, and I felt I would lose a friend if I let her go. But I knew I must step out of her world and back into my own life. I had done my best to share Priscilla's message to the world. So, on with my own world of painting and art, or so I thought.

Weeks passed. One day I received a phone invitation from my old friend Edith to visit with her at her family homestead in New Hampshire. I had not seen her for many years. I remembered when she and I were teenagers, we spent a very cold New Hampshire day nestled down in a warm mountainous pile of sawdust at the family's sawmill. The biting cold could only reach our noses. My bedroom had a real feather bed, the first I had ever slept in. Attached to the house, there was a shed where all manner of old things were kept. These thoughts were with me as my husband and I drove to their New Hampshire woods. Hours later, we were again in that same bedroom. It seemed smaller, but the same bed was still there. The next morning after a visit to the sawmill, I mentioned the old shed to Edith and the memorable treasures it once held. "Let's explore it again," I said.

As I had anticipated, it was still filled with relics of the past. There were *National Geographic* magazines and an old trunk filled with black clothes, probably used for funerals. Old tools were scattered on a workbench. Funny rusted skates hung from the wall. There were a few enameled pans and a bookcase with old books. A beautiful red bound book with gold lettering caught my eye. It was dated 1893 and titled *Pagan and Christian Rome* by Rodolfo Lanciani. It was devoted to the tombs of Rome, as well as to Christian cemeteries, and the title page claimed it was "profusely illustrated."

This book turned out to be a true treasure for it had pages of information about the famous archaeologist Giovanni Battista de Rossi and his rediscovery of the catacombs of Priscilla in the late 1800s. He wrote that two of the homes in Rome where Peter and Paul found hospitality were those of the Pudens family and of Priscilla and Aquila. It seemed that Priscilla had followed me even to New Hampshire!

There was no doubt in my mind of the gift I wanted from this old house and hoped my friend would oblige. Apparently, God was not through with me and my research about Priscilla. If the truth were known, I was thrilled to be again searching for additional proof of Priscilla's legacy.

A few hours spent with this newly acquired volume yielded some fascinating information. Rodolfo Lanciani, the author of my recent acquisition, stated that the Priscilla catacomb was in use during the second through fourth centuries. Antonio Bosio, considered the Columbus of the Catacombs, uncovered it in the late 1500s. It had been sealed since around AD 500, probably to protect it from vandalism or to avoid the spread of diseases. In 1776, a man named Carrara discovered a chapel that was later found to be a part of the Priscilla catacomb.

Among my slides was one with 1777 written in graffiti high on the wall in the catacomb. According to Lanciani, no attention was paid to this discovery in spite of its potential importance. He indicated that the only record of it was on a scrap of paper in codex 9697 in the Bibliothèque nationale in Paris.[54] Most intriguing were Lanciani's comments about a secret or treasure buried in the Priscilla catacombs. He told about the destruction of the catacombs during many excavations as people looked for its secret.

> *When did this wholesale destruction take place? In times much nearer ours than the reader may imagine, I have been able to ascertain the date, with the help of an anecdote related by Pietro Sante Bartoli in #144 of his archaeological memoirs: "Excavations were made under Innocent X (1634–1655), and Clement IX (1667–1670), in the Monte delle Gioe, on via*

Salaria, with the hope of discovering a certain hidden treasure.
The hope was frustrated; but, deep in the bowels of the mound,
some crypts were found, encrusted with white stucco, and
remarkable for their neatness and preservation.[55]

What was this hidden treasure to which he alluded? What were they searching for? Lanciani went on to say the following:

There is no doubt that the anecdote refers to the tomb of Acilii
Glabriones, which is cut under Monte delle Gioe, and is the
only one in the Catacombs of Priscilla remarkable for a coating
of white stucco. Its destruction, therefore, took place under
Clement IX, and was the work of treasure hunters. And the
very nature of clandestine excavations, which are the work of
malicious, ignorant, and suspicious persons, explains the reason
why no mention of the discovery was made to contemporary
archaeologists', and the pleasure of rediscovering the secret of the
Acilii Glabriones was reserved for us.[56]

Over the centuries, many archaeologists and treasure hunters excavated the catacombs, looking for secrets and treasures. Archaeologist Giovanni Battista de Rossi believed that it was more than just an old Roman nobleman's tomb, that it had hidden secrets, and that Priscilla's catacomb was haunted. Why did the popes Innocent X and Clement IX suspect that there was a secret buried there? None of the excavators found any secret treasures. Their eyes were seeking tangible, earthly riches. The real treasure hidden in Priscilla's catacomb was an important spiritual one that documented the foundation of the new Christian faith: the world's oldest Marian painting and a sky chart recording the birth date of the Savior.

Discovering Lanciani's book reenergized my efforts to prove Priscilla's authorship. One problem that continued to nag at me was that some scholars seemed to say, "Give us another book of the Bible for a woman to have written, not The Letter to the Hebrews. That is the epistle of priesthood. Therefore, a woman could not have written it." I continued to research the times in which Priscilla lived. Bits and pieces of information helped me form a clearer picture. There were references to Montanism, which particularly excited me because women were leaders in this group within the early Christian church.

The frescoed portrait that I photographed in the Priscilla catacomb of a female leader with her hands up in prayer perplexed me. When I first had seen it, I believed it was Priscilla, but several book references to the fresco describe her as just an orant. Though I found other references

Orant in prayer

stating that Antonio Bosio, the archaeologist, believed this orant was Saint Priscilla Matrona, founder of the cemetery.[57] I believed this fresco was of Saint Priscilla, confidante of Paul and wife of Aquila.

In the fresco, she was wearing a white shawl and purple robes. Why was her clothing so much different from the other paintings of people of her time? I also still had unanswered questions as to why there was a discrepancy in The Letter to the Hebrews' description of the furnishing in the Holy of Holies from that in the Old Testament.

With these questions in mind, I was referred to Rabbi Arthur Chiel, a most pleasant, helpful, and knowledgeable man. He was the rabbi of Congregation B'nai Jacob in Woodbridge, Connecticut. When Rabbi Chiel saw the picture of Priscilla in her robe praying, he said, "This is impossible, a woman wearing a rabbinical shawl two thousand years ago!" He became as interested as I and wanted a copy, which I gave him. He wanted to send it to the Jewish Museum in New York.

I told him about my belief in Priscilla's authorship and that I had found a discrepancy in The Letter to the Hebrews. It concerned the description of the Holy of Holies. He thought the author of The Letter to the Hebrews was just taking poetic license. He took out a miniature model of the Holy of Holies. I peered down into the model and could see the parts that were not as she described. As a Christian priest, she would have led services in her own home. As a traditional Jewish woman, she would not have been allowed into a temple's Holy of Holies. If a male religious leader were the author to The Letter to the Hebrews, he would not have made this mistake.

The early church was filled with women in leadership positions. They were ordained as deacons, priests, and bishops. This practice was continued for several centuries, including in the New Prophecy sect (later called Montanism) founded in the mid-second century by two women and a man: Priscilla, Maximilla, and Montanus. The relationship of the Priscilla of the New Prophecy to the Priscilla married to Aquila is unknown. This early form of worship had as a tenet that Christians should die for their faith instead of fleeing persecution. Priscilla and Aquila were both martyred for their faith, perhaps inspiring this later group.

Another of the New Prophecy's beliefs was that Christians who had sinned or apostatized[58] were unable to return to grace and were forever damned.[59] As I mulled over this information, I began to have the feeling that I had read something similar in The Letter to the Hebrews.

For it is impossible to restore again to repentance those who
have once been enlightened, who have tasted the heavenly gift,
and become partakers of the Holy Spirit, and have tasted the
goodness of the word of God and the powers of the age to come.
(Heb. 6:4–5)[60]

The New Prophecy movement came less than a hundred years after The Letter to the Hebrews was written and seems to have many parallels with the Hebrews' new covenant (the later church declared Montanism heretical).

I wondered if the issue of apostatizing was close to Priscilla's personal life. There are several records indicating that Aquila of Sinope (perhaps her son or grandson) apostatized, possibly to follow his interest in astrology. Those who followed the stars in those days were punished by Roman law and would have had to apostatize or renounce their Christian beliefs.

Slowly things were falling into place, and Priscilla was emerging as the central figure I had believed her to be at the beginning of my quest. In order for her to wear a rabbinical shawl, she must have been a rabbi or priest in the early church. In such a role, she would be in position to preach the truth as she understood it and to teach it to Apollos and other Christians. What better way to advance Christianity and spread her teaching than to record her preaching in her letter to the Hebrews? Yet while much of early Christianity was accepting of women's leadership, this was not the case across most of the ancient world. The letter to the Hebrews would not have been as widely accepted if it were clearly signed by a woman.

Perhaps there was more to the saga of Priscilla, but I had the feeling that my mission was nearly over. As I prayed throughout this strange experience for continued guidance, so did I also pray for continued help in making Priscilla's story known to more than just the few individuals with whom I had personal contact. While my discovery of the apple constellation had been widely published, little of my revelation about Priscilla's authorship had been included.

I recalled four words from the first time Priscilla entered my life more than a year earlier: *conception, creation, revelation,* and *reflection.*

Her message was *conceived* and then *created* in her letter to the Hebrews. Now it had been *revealed* to us in the context of her life. It is for us, the living, to *reflect* in our lives the faith for which she lived and died. I was grateful that God permitted me to serve as her messenger. It was appropriate that God, in his great wisdom, chose our day and age to reveal Priscilla as one of his priests in the early Christian church and as the author of The Letter to the Hebrews. The Western world would now have a greater understanding that God loves women's leadership as much as that of men.

CHAPTER ELEVEN

God Doesn't Call the Qualified; He Qualifies the Called

It was easy to point to a sky chart and a frescoed apple tree and have people see the connection. But I had many more points connecting Priscilla to her authorship of The Letter to the Hebrews. Yet people were less willing to see, and publishers less willing to take such a stand. In moments of discouragement, I would ask, "Why me?" I would ask that of myself, as well as hear that question from others. I would cry inside for the right answer, but I never doubted Priscilla's authorship.

Everyone needs time for reflection, and I had always found peace and the opportunity for introspection when our family returned to its old stomping grounds in Brewster on Cape Cod. Walking out onto the tidal flats, where, only hours before, the water had been deep, always seemed sacred. It felt like the receding waters had washed away all that was before. As the first to press feet into the newly revealed sand, I felt a renewal.

On one of these walks out on the sandbars, my eldest daughter, Bonnie, asked me to tell her the whole story of my year with Priscilla's spirit. She had often seen me deep in research but had only heard fragments of my story while I was flying in and out of doors on my quest. Now we had time to talk, with only the seagulls to interrupt us.

"Is it over, Mom?" she asked. I could only answer an ineffective, "I don't know." I should have known it would never be truly over. Then she asked if I realized this revelation had begun with a color spectrum star design and then led to a whole constellation of stars!

Sometimes I cannot see what is under my very nose. No, I had not realized it until she mentioned it. But it made me summarize the entire experience. It began with a tremendous inspiration that revealed hidden facts on art, religion, archaeology, and science and that finally carried me back into history to reveal Priscilla's priesthood. All with the veil of the Spirit drawing each together by their interactions, making it difficult to know where one ended and the other began through time and space.

Was my mission over? One last letter from Priscilla came through me. I kept a pad and pencil beside my bed for the creative thoughts that came to me at night. One morning, after I had put some things away, I picked up the notes that I had scribbled during the night. Having lived and communicated with Priscilla's spirit these many months, I had felt her and her descendants reach out to me. I imagined their message if they were to write to us in one voice in a letter today:

> *It was not easy to have Carolyn as a messenger. She had to be continually reassured in her mission. The severity of my letter to the Hebrews left no tolerance for those who had fallen from grace. The severity of the environment in our day demanded it. The strength that it demanded of us also reached through time to sustain her.*
>
> *The first church in Rome, at my home, respected my teaching the words of the Lord. Through my tutelage, Paul, Apollos, my son, Linus, and many others grew in knowledge, discipline, and love, which supported them in their faith and in their martyrdom. Our early descendants in the faith continued to spread the new covenant, and I was honored in life and in death. Popes, bishops, and martyrs were buried in my catacomb. But four hundred years after my death, the Church of Rome declared many of my followers in Christ heretics but sainted me!*
>
> *We early believers were tested to the utmost, for we were known as the purest of Christ's followers. We had Roman law to persecute us, we had other Jewish sects with which to contend, and we incurred the wrath of pagans. Many followers apostatized for they could not bear the punishment nor witness*

the punishment of others—a test of our faith. But the crushing agony of spirit came when our own church declared us heretics in AD 380, issuing the edict on the Catholic faith, which states the following:

> *We ordain that the name of Catholic Christians shall apply to all those who obey the present law. All others we judge to be mad and demented. We declare them guilty of the infamy of holding heretical doctrine.*

Bishops tried to cast the demon (demon derived from the Greek daimonion, *meaning "a thing of divine nature") from my descendant and namesake, but she left Rome for her ancestral home in Pontus. She cried to them, "I am not the wolf but the lamb!"[61] All my children's children and thereafter believed in me and carried on my name as a symbol of their inheritance. It was not our enemies we needed to fear but our friends, for as early as AD 398, they had written the following:*

> *Clerics adhering to the Eunomian or Montanist superstition shall be excluded from all intercourse within the city or town, let them be sent in to perpetual exile . . . their books of their teachings, be sought out and burnt with fire under the eyes of the magistrates. Should anyone conceal these harmful books he shall suffer capital punishment.*

Can we ever be redeemed by the church? No one should judge the right or wrong of others' beliefs. The importance of this living religion is reflected in its meaningful actions, not in its judgments. For purity is harmonious.

> *You will see visions with your pure heart and turning your face downward you will even hear manifestations of voices saluting you with its secrets.[62]*

We are made from all our ancestors, who passed before us. Not only in our appearance but also in our thoughts and values. And we are further shaped by the environs in which we live.

I thought my service was over, but Carolyn rattled my bones, as I did hers, for heaven does not stand still. Did you think it did? Heaven is the other end of the pattern of life where it empties into a continuing flow of fulfillments of timeless joy upon entering back into God. Your bodily death cannot stop you from your growing spirit. There is another dimension in time and space, which scientists recognize today. It would have been difficult in my time to comprehend.

There is nothing left of my world except what you call ancient ruins: the Coliseum, the Appian Way, a few walls, and our tombs. Those are physical things of no worth. Even the temple that my grandson Aquila helped Hadrian to build is gone. (He had continued in his father's ways.) Everything is gone. So too will a few walls be all that is left of your world in two thousand years. My age left you the inheritance of our ideals and our faith, which need no walls. Will you leave the same?

God is with you always.

Priscilla

CHAPTER TWELVE

Back to Rome

Once more I opened Priscilla's letter to the Hebrews, to her special chapter 11 verse 3, where I had found so many clues that had led me on. It seemed every time I read it, something new would reveal itself. Again I read Hebrews 11:3.

> *By faith, by believing in God, we know that the world and the stars, in fact all things were made at God's command and that they were all made from things that can't be seen.*[63]

Without a moment of hesitation, I turned back to the Old Testament and found Deuteronomy 32:10–11. (Was I being led again?)

> *God protected Israel in the howling wilderness as though they were the* apple *of His eye. He spread His wings over Israel even as an* eagle *overspreads her young.*[64]

This imagery is repeated in the catacomb. For the constellation of Aquila (Latin for *eagle*) was spread over Israel when Christ was born. And the eagle constellation was disguised as apples down in Priscilla's catacombs.

Numerous connections between Priscilla, The Letter to the Hebrews, and the Old Testament are illustrated in her catacomb.

In The Letter to the Hebrews, she wrote the following:

It was faith that brought the walls of Jericho tumbling down.[65]

I turned again to the Old Testament to read about Joshua entering Jericho and came across Joshua 4:19:

On the tenth day of the first month the people went up from the Jordon and camped at Gilgal on the eastern border of the Jericho. [66]

"The tenth day of the first month" meant nothing to me. I soon found, though, that the tenth day of the first month in the Hebrew calendar corresponds to the middle of the month of March in our modern calendar. Quite close to the March 24–25 date recorded in Priscilla's catacomb!

My discovery of the secret sky chart painted nearly two thousand years ago still seemed so unbelievable to me. Especially the fact that I had been the one to find it! I needed to see it again.

This time I made better advance preparations for Rome. Letters were sent and answered, and arrangements were made. I would not have the same innocence this time, but neither would I have the same support and comfort of friends as I had before. Many would not be there. Two had died. Others were helping in a leper colony in Central America, and still others were in Africa, Australia, South America, and the Philippines. Only Sister Charles, the librarian, had remained. I would be on my own but more so since I would not have my friend and guide, Henri. Rome would not be the same.

As part of my advance preparations, I met with the Episcopal bishop of Connecticut, Morgan Porteus. He received me in his office and listened intently to my story of Priscilla. He kindly asked how he might help. I appealed to him to help open doors as I returned to Rome.

A few days later, our parish priest called on us at home. I told him I was planning to return to Rome and asked if he could come to my assistance? He dialed up his friend E. A. Bayne (Ned), who, on the other end, laughingly explained that he had just mailed Carolyn a letter offering his service because of a request he got from the bishop.

Ned Bayne had connections in Rome as he was part of the American Universities Field Staff. He had been serving with the American college and university programs in Italy. Doors seemed to be opening!

Lunching with Dorrit Hoffleit, the astronomer, I mentioned I was going back to Rome. She inquired if I was planning to visit with the pope's astronomer. I thought she was joking and gave a flippant response. But she was serious. What, I wondered, was the pope doing with an astronomer? Earlier, popes publicly disclaimed astronomers, like Kepler and Galileo. Even my ancient friend Aquila of Sinope had to hide his knowledge of astronomy down in his family catacomb. Dorrit assured me that Pope John Paul II did have an astronomer, and if I would like to meet him, she would arrange it. Father Martin McCarthy had once been a student of hers at Harvard before becoming a Jesuit priest and astronomer in Rome. He would, she felt, be most interested in my discovery.

Father McCarthy's invitation arrived! I was to visit him at the pope's summer palace in Castel Gandolfo. More doors were opening! Things seemed to be falling in place, but I still had no idea what I might find. My anticipation was a mixture of enthusiasm and uncertainty.

Arriving in Rome, I settled in at a small hotel near the Pantheon that had been recommended by Ned Bayne's secretary. I was very lucky to have this place to stay. The Synod of Bishops was in session, and all of Rome was filled with priests, bishops, and their entourages from all over the world. People often avoid visiting Rome during these events for accommodations are nearly impossible. I hadn't known this.

The day before my visit to the pope's summer palace, I was a guest speaker at St. Paul's within the Walls. I mentioned to the rector, Father Wilbur C. Woodhams, my invitation to Castel Gandolfo for the following day. He explained the problems I would encounter trying to reach the palace. I would have to transfer several times between buses and switch to a new metro system, all the while not being able to speak Italian. It would be nearly impossible. Before I became too anxious, he offered to drive me there.

In my naivety, I had not known about the near impossibility of getting accommodations or the difficult transportation to Castel Gandolfo. Of course, not knowing something is nearly impossible can often make things possible! God's grace and the graciousness of others continued to open doors.

My day ended with a meeting with the renowned Mme Margherita Guarducci, the archaeologist who discovered St. Peter's bones hidden under the Basilica of St. Peter. We were able to share my research and discoveries in spite of our language barrier.

The next day, as I stepped out of Father Woodham's car in front of Castel Gandolfo's double doors, a handsome, jolly-faced priest came through them and grasped my hands in a warm welcome. Father Martin McCarthy was a giant of a man with a Bostonian Irish grin cracking through his smooth round cheeks. We spent a beautiful and informative day together, beginning on the roof of the palace, where we could look down on Lake Albano.

The greater the person, the more understanding they are. Father McCarthy was very encouraging about my research. I had been prepared for an argument or a condescending attitude from such a leader in the field of astronomy. Instead, he was enthused about my discoveries and told me that one of the craters on the moon was named Priscilla for an astronomer of that name. After tea, a man in a tuxedo came into the room carrying the pope's guest book for me to sign. I was invited to sit at the pope's large carved desk in the center of the parlor. The first signatures in the book were from 1906. It held the signatures of all the popes and their notable guests from that year forward. Father McCarthy, handing me a pen, pointed out the signatures of Queen Elizabeth, the astronomer Hubble, and many others. I was deeply honored when he asked me to add my signature. He also allowed me to hold the moon rock that President Nixon had presented to the pope as a gift from the American people.

At the end of this late autumn day, we walked into the pope's private garden, where a small Roman amphitheater had recently been uncovered in the hillside. Thousands of wild flowers strategically planted near the pool among statues and precisely trimmed trees created a sense of informality in the formal gardens. I picked one of the flowers and later pressed it in my address book. We stood on a balcony that jutted out over a cliff to view the sunset.

Father McCarthy at Vatican Observatory

Father McCarthy said that this garden once belonged to an emperor who had designed it so that the sun would shine on him long after the city below was in darkness. I watched the sinking sun's orange glow reflect on his face as he spoke.

It was a day I shall always treasure. I went away from this day with a pressed purple flower, a few photos, and priceless memories. As we parted, Father McCarthy pointed to an early group of evening stars and mentioned that these were the Pleiades, a group of stars I was to encounter again soon!

My last days in Rome were spent down in Priscilla's catacomb. This time, a professional photographer named Bini accompanied me. Mme Sophie Chandler Consagra, the director of the American Academy in Rome, had arranged the photographer. Armed with a handwritten letter from Father Umberto Fasola, the director of the catacombs, I had the permission and access I needed to study the hidden sky chart more closely.

Our guide, Sister Maria Francesca, Bini, and I were not down in the catacomb very long before the lights went out. My first thought in the darkness was of the last time I was there—how the lights had gone out, my new Eveready flashlight died, and my camera jammed. Sister Maria began to make her way with her flashlight through the labyrinth of blackened passageways to restore the lights. Was I in for the same annoying situation? Good thing, I thought, that I was not superstitious.

Fortunately, Bini had brought a flashlight, knowing that the lighting was usually very dim. While we waited for Sister Maria to restore the lights, I borrowed Bini's flashlight and investigated some narrow side tunnels. I was not frightened but comfortable and curious.

Once the lights were restored, I was able to see the apple tree fresco and study the far side of its cracked ceiling. I saw six more faded apples

in an S pattern, which I had not noticed two years earlier. These apples (more disguised stars) were on the extreme left branches of the painted fruit tree. Part of the left side of the fresco was missing, where the plaster had broken and fallen away. Bini carefully took photos for my later study. More stars for me to decipher when I got home.

The only friend still remaining in Rome from my previous visit was Sister Charles Marie, the librarian, whom I saw when I visited the library. I mentioned to her my difficulties not being able to speak Italian and the expense of living in a hotel and eating in restaurants. She invited me to stay at her home on the top floor of an apartment building. She also took me to the market and taught me how the Italians buy their fresh food so I would not always have to eat out. She was a gentle, kind angel whose hospitality I cherished.

Sister Charles Marie also introduced me to a spirited American archaeologist, Alice Mulhern, whose recent retirement gave her the hours to read excerpts to me from the old Italian books stored at the Germanica Bibliothek. She was another angel coming to my rescue at the right time and right place. Alice would later translate *Guide to the Catacombs of Priscilla* by Sandro Carletti for publishing by the Vatican. I never could have gleaned any information from these voluminous tomes written in old Italian and/or Latin without her. I couldn't even read the modern Italian language. Such audacity for me to even be in the same room with those unreadable books!

One day in the library, as I was waiting for Alice, I stopped by a shelf where there was a set of books titled *The Beginnings of Christianity*. After having been immersed for several days in old Italian books, I was surprised to see and read words in English. I opened *Part I: the Acts of the Apostles: Vol. IV Translation and Commentary* by Kirsopp Lake and searched its pages for Priscilla's name. Part of the commentary acknowledged a well-recognized hypothesis that Priscilla was "a woman of great importance in the early church, and may have written the Epistle to the Hebrews."

Rendel Harris, von Harnack, Ruth Hoppin, M. J. Shroyer, and others had all thought as I did. I wondered how they had come to their conclusions. Did each of them have a revelation, like I did, and set out to prove it? What did each of us know that the others did not? If all these scholars, much more learned than I, knew this, why wasn't it universally known? I supposed that I must accept the fact that there would always be some who would not acknowledge the truth about a woman writing part of the Bible. In spite of the evidence, they would deny it or, at best, dismiss it by saying, "What difference does it make who wrote the books of the Bible?"

But it does make a difference. It is important! Why else are there books named Mark, Matthew, Luke, John, Timothy, Peter, James, Titus, and Philemon? I believe it should be shouted from the rooftops, "Look at yourselves, women! Look what we have done! You not only have the seed of life, but you have a brain too! A woman was inspired to write a book of the Bible! Who knows, maybe more than one!"

After I arrived home back in the United States, I studied the photographs from when Bini and I went down into the catacombs. I was able to see that the six extra stars beyond the damaged part of the fresco matched part of the Pleiades star cluster. The entire catacomb sky chart fresco, from right to left, showed the following: Madonna and child, the constellation Aquila over the Madonna's head, the Northern Cross (Cygnus), Pegasus, Andromeda spanning the repaired portion of the ceiling, more damaged cracks, and finally, six stars in the Pleiades. The Pleiades were the star cluster Father McCarthy had pointed out in the evening sky as I left Castel Gandolfo. I believe he had known that I would see them again in the catacomb.

EPILOGUE

As I looked back over my journey of more than a year with Priscilla, I tried to make sense of it all. I had experienced all manner of emotional highs and lows, moments when I felt strongly driven by the spirit and others when I was at a complete loss for motivation and direction. At every turn, especially when I was unsure, earthly angels would appear, open doors, smooth my path, and spur me on. It was clear to me from the beginning that I was being divinely led for a purpose.

My spiritual and intellectual journey with Priscilla had ranged across the disciplines of art, literature, history, religion, archeology, astronomy, and physics. I had traveled to the jungles of Puerto Rico to see the world's largest radio telescope, into the bowels of the earth below the Vatican to see St. Peter's burial place, into a catacomb to see and connect even more with my spiritual guide, and to the pope's summer palace to meet his astronomer.

It all began with a revelation that called for faith. The year of searching for confirmation and proof of Priscilla's authorship had shown me that I was not alone in my belief. Though far from being a scholar, I had been driven to do things and go places I never would have on my own. God placed me, with my artist's eye, thousands of miles from home and hundreds of feet below the ground to reveal a message that many had seen but none had understood. This discovery provided another important link between Priscilla and her leadership role in early Christianity. Yet it was not the confirmation and proof that I thought I had been searching for.

If I were being divinely led for a purpose, what could that purpose have been? I had believed it was to prove Priscilla's authorship of The Letter to the Hebrews, something I still believed and would continue to believe for all my days. Perhaps such definitive proof does not exist, or if it did, the world would still not be ready to accept it. Such proof could be in too much danger of being denied, suppressed, or even destroyed by a still male-dominated church.

Perhaps the reason for my journey was to discover the hidden sky chart or to interact, influence, and be influenced by all the marvelous people I met along the way. My purpose could have been the journey itself. Or perhaps, this was all about transforming me, a holiday Christian, into a woman of deeper faith through revelation, inspiration, and reflection.

I never again saw my friend Henri Nouwen, the most spiritual and saintly man I had ever met. He had finished his tenure at Yale and returned for some time to a life of contemplation and worship at the Abbey of the Genesee. He took only a few possessions with him, including my painting of the frog that listened to a different drummer. Henri died in September of 1996.

The painting given to Henri

The location of the painting is now unknown. Whenever I thought of Henri or my spiritual journey with Priscilla, I was glad that I too had heard a different drummer. Sometimes marching to that beat is the journey God wants for us.

10-3-79

Dear Carolyn,

Many thanks for your good
letter. I very much hope that "proof
of the beginning" will be published.
I look forward to the time when the
aipplane stewardess will ask me on the
way to Holland:"What do you like to
read Esquire or Smithonian?" I then
will have no problem deciding!

But.... if it all falls trhough,
I hope you keep smiling and do not feel
dejected. Here in the monastery I see
better then wherever that what really
counts is God's marvelous work with
us and that from that perspective we
can enjoy our many decorations of life
but do not have to be too startled when
they fall off the ceiling once and a while.

How good to hear that you are
back to painting. I hope you can stay
with it, even when a new studio is not
realistic. You have so much to give
through your paintings that I hope and

pray that even Priscilla will not pull you
away from your easel.

Life here is very good for me. I enjoy
the opportunity to"taste and see"how good the
Lord is, to spend many hours in prayer, to
listen to the readings, to study the Russian
Mystics and to think about that famous question,
why I am brought into this world and what I
have done with my life so far and what I still
can do with it, or better: what God wants me to
do with it.

I hope you like thenew paintings I bought
in Rome and that you can help Jane to put them
up in my office. I am very fond of them. Their
brightness and naivite attracts me very much.

Keep me in your prayers and try to find
some time in your day to be with the Lord and
him alone. He wants always to show you his love.

Yours,
peace,

CAMBRIDGE, MASSACHUSETTS 02138
March 7, 1983

Carolyn Beehler
845 Whitney Avenue
New Haven, Connecticut 06511

Dear Carolyn,

Thanks so much for your wonderful letter. It was a joy to hear from you again and, especially to realize that you have kept your joyful, playful and humorous spirit in the midst of all your struggles.

Thanks so much for writing me about your cancer of the bladder. I really am grateful that you told me about this and about your response to it. I am so grateful for your vitality and joy. Be sure that I will keep you very close in my prayers and thoughts and also be sure that the spirit of hope and joy is much stronger than any bodily enemy.

I hope especially that you find yourself growingly in love with the God who has created us and set us free and who wants to love us with a zealous love. I think it is the knowledge of this first love that has the power to destroy the forces of destruction and death. Jesus said, "In the world, you will have trouble but be of good cheer; I have overcome the world." Let these be consoling and comforting words for you.

I am very excited that your theory is getting around the world. It certainly deserves it. I still remember very vividly when you first told me about your great discovery and I am still excited about it and often tell it to friends. It belongs to one of the most precious stories I know.

Meanwhile, I have been trying to get to know the whole new world here at Harvard. It certainly is a very different place than Yale. In many ways, tougher and more distant and harder to enter into. But also quite challenging and with many wonderful and creative people. It is probably going to take quite a while before I can call this my "home" but I think it is worth the effort.

With love,

Henri Nouwen

P.S. Warm greetings to Dan.

Carolyn, author

Carolyn M. Beehler

The difficult plight of being an artist is removing oneself from the ordinary life to hunt down a vision that will enhance the lives of others.

Carolyn Beehler had a lifelong affair with art. An award-winning watercolorist, she was also a sculptor, worked in acrylics, and was an occasional poet and author. A highly regarded art teacher and lecturer, she taught from her studio, led classes across New England, and was an instructor at the Lay School of Religion at the Yale Divinity School. She was a native of New Haven, Connecticut, a graduate of the Paier School of Art, a member of the New Haven Brush and Palette Club, and was on the board of the Hamden Arts Council. Carolyn also served as the art director for Yale's Starlight Festival.

Her paintings are in the permanent collections of the Mattatuck Museum, the New Hampshire Audubon, the US Coast Guard, and many commercial and private collections in the United States and abroad.

As a result of her Priscilla revelation and discoveries, Carolyn lectured at venues such as the Yale Divinity School, St. Paul's within the Walls in Rome, and Rensselaer Polytechnic Institute. In 1980, the pope's astronomer invited her to Castel Gandolfo, Italy, to acknowledge, discuss, and congratulate her for her discovery of the hidden sky chart in the Priscilla catacomb. *Smithsonian* magazine, *United Church of Christ AD* magazine, the University of Maryland's journal *Archaeoastronomy*, and many newspapers published articles about her discovery of the Christmas star chart. One of her television interviews is still available for viewing on YouTube, "The Priscilla Revelation & the Christmas Star."

In 1997, she and her husband moved from New Haven to Tucson, Arizona, where she continued to lecture about her revelation and discoveries and to be an award-winning painter. Carolyn passed away in January of 2006.

NOTES

Chapter Two

1   John Mason, *Believe You Can* (Revell, 2004), 199.
2   Holy Bible containing the Old and New Testaments, King James Version (El Reno, Oklahoma: Rainbow Studies Inc, 1981, 1986, 1989), 1433–1443.

Chapter Three

3   Frederick Carl Eiselen, Edwin Lewis, and David G. Downey, *The Abingdon Bible Commentary* (The Abingdon Press, 1929), 1295–1326.
4   Hampton Keathley IV, "The Argument of Hebrews," August 12, 2004, accessed August 8, 2014, http://bible.org/article/argument-hebrews.
5   *Encyclopædia Britannica Online,* s.v. "Tertullian."
6   Michal Hunt, "The Letter to the Hebrews: Introduction," 2007, http://www.agapebiblestudy.com/hebrews/Hebrews_Introduction.htm.
7   Hunt, "Letter to the Hebrews."
8   James E. Kiefer, "Jerome, Scholar, Translator and Theologian," Biographical Sketches of Memorable Christians of the Past, accessed October 16, 2014, http://justus.anglican.org/resources/bio/256.html.
9   Hunt, "Letter to the Hebrews."
10 Timothy J. Finney, "The Letter to the Hebrews," accessed August 8, 2014.
11 Eiselen, Lewis, and Downey, *Abingdon Bible Commentary,* 1297.
12 John W. Ritenbaugh, "Suntheke," Forerunner Commentary, accessed April 27, 2015, www.Bibletools.org, accessed.

13 The Bible, Revised Standard Version (New York: American Bible Society, 1952, 1946, 1971), 965.

14 The International Version of the Holy Bible (Grand Rapids, Michigan: Zondervan Publishing House, 173, 1978, 184), 1725.

15 Ibid., 1726.

16 Ibid., 1768.

17 Ibid., 1793.

18 Ibid., 1856.

19 Peter Joseph Chandlery, *Pilgrim-Walks in Rome: A Guide to the Holy Places* (London: Forgotten Books, 1903), 98–99.

20 Chandlery, *Pilgrim-Walks*.

21 Robert D. Mock, MD, "The Manuscript and Mural Evidence for the Synagogue of the Nazarenes: Study into the Archeology and History of the Hebrew Nazarene Synagogue Called by Christians the Apostolic Church in the House with the Upper Room," September 2004, accessed August 8, 2014, www.biblesearchers.com/hebrewchurch/synagogue/synagogue4.shtml.

22 Ruth Hoppin, *Priscilla's Letter: Finding the Author of the Epistle to the Hebrews* (Lost Coast Press, 1997), 98–99.

23 Henry D. M. Spence-Jones, MA, DD, dean of Gloucester, *The Early Christians in Rome* (John Lane Company, January 1911), 265–266.

24 The Bible containing the Old and New Testaments, Revised Standard Version (New York: American Bible Society, 1946, 1952, 1971), 1048.

25 Ibid.

26 Ibid.

27 Ibid.

28 Ibid., 1049.

29 Ibid., 1049.

30 Ibid., 1051.

31 Ibid., 1053.

32 Ibid.

33 Holy Bible containing the Old and New Testaments, King James Version (El Reno, Oklahoma: Rainbow Studies, Inc., 1981, 1986, 1989), 1445.

34 The Bible containing the Old and New Testaments, Revised Standard Version (New York: American Bible Society, 1946, 1952, 1971), 1051.

35 Ibid.

36 Ibid., 1048.

37 Ibid., 82.

38 Ibid., 83.

39 Ibid.

Chapter Four

40 David Wallechinsky and Irving Wallace, "She Wrote It, He Got the Credit: Women Writing for Men; St. Paul Epistle to the Hebrews and Priscilla," accessed August 8, 2014, www.trivia-library.com/.../**women-writing-for-men-st-paul-epistle-to-the**..Hebrews.

41 Pierre M. Du Bourguet, SJ, *The Art of the Copts*, trans. Caryll Hay-Shaw (New York: Crown Publishers Inc., 1967–1971), 85.

42 Randall Price, *Secrets of the Dead Sea Scrolls* (Eugene, Oregon: World of Bible Ministries, 1996), 43.

Chapter Five

43 A. Waal, "Roman Catacombs," *The Catholic Encyclopedia* (New York: Robert Appleton Company, 1908), accessed August 14, 2014, http://www.newadvent.org/cathen/03417b.htm.

44 Rev. J. Spencer Northcoate and Rev. W. R. Brownlow, *Roma Sotterranea: Some Accounts of the Roman Catacombs* (London: Longmans, Green, Reader and Dyer, 1869), 5–7.

45 O. Marucchi, trans., *Christian Epigraphy: An Elementary Treatise* (Cambridge: Cambridge University Press, 1912), 241.

46 Hoppin, *Priscilla's Letter*, 97.

47 "Significance of Halos," Catholic Tradition, accessed February 6, 2015, www.catholictradition.org/saints/halos.htm.

Chapter Six

48 Photo of Santa Prassede, mosaic over door inside chapel of St. Zeno, http://www.sacred-destinations.com/italy/rome-santa=prassede/photo/eos_143.

49 Spence-Jones, *Early Christians in Rome*, 264–265.

50 Ibid.

51 Ibid.

[52] The Bible containing the Old and New Testaments, Revised Standard Version (New York: American Bible Society, 1946, 1952, 1971), 1050.

Chapter Nine

[53] Dorrit Hoffleit, "The Christmas Star, Novae, and Pulsars," *the Journal for the American Association of Variable Star Observers* 13, no.1 (June 1984): 15–20.

Chapter Ten

[54] Rodolfo Lanciani, *Pagan and Christian Rome* (Cambridge: The Riverside Press, 1893), 111.

[55] Ibid., 8.

[56] Ibid., 9.

[57] Mary M. Shaefer, *Women in Pastoral Office: The Story of Santa Prassede Rome* (Oxford: Oxford University Press, 2013), 190.

[58] Collins English Dictionary, s.v. "apostatized."

[59] Glenn Davis, "The Development of the Canon of the New Testament: Montanism and Montanus 2–3 century," 1997–2010, accessed August 16, 2014 http://www.ntcanon.org/Montanism.shtml.

[60] The Bible containing the Old and New Testaments, Revised Standard Version (New York: American Bible Society, 1946, 1952, 1971), 1046.

Chapter Eleven

[61] Robert M. Grant, *Second Century Christianity: A Collection of Fragments* (Louisville, Kentucky: Westminster John Knox Press, 2003), 41.

[62] Grant, *Second Century Christianity*.

Chapter Twelve

[63] *The Living Bible* (Carol Stream, Illinois: Tyndale House Publishers Inc., 1971).

[64] Ibid.

[65] The Bible containing the Old and New Testaments, Revised Standard Version (New York, American Bible Society, 1946, 1952, 1971), 1051.

[66] The International Version of the Holy Bible (Grand Rapids, Michigan: Zondervan Publishing House, 173, 1978, 184), 336.

Printed in the United States
By Bookmasters